**Consumer Reports**

# The
# Best
# of
# Health

Marvin M. Lipman, M.D.,
and the Editors of
Consumer Reports on Health

**Consumer Reports Best of Health** is published by Consumers Union, the nonprofit organization that publishes CONSUMER REPORTS, the monthly magazine of test reports, product Ratings, and buying guidance. Established in 1936, Consumers Union is chartered under the Not-for-Profit Corporation Law of the State of New York. Standard postage paid at Yonkers, NY, and at other mailing offices. Canadian postage paid at Mississauga, Ontario, Canada. Canadian publications registration no. 2665247-98. **U.S. Postmaster:** Send address changes to P.O. Box 2109, Harlan, IA 51593-0298. Canada Post: If copies are undeliverable, return to CONSUMER REPORTS, P.O. Box 1051, STN MAIN, Fort Erie ON L2A 6C7.

The information contained in this book is not intended to substitute for professional or medical advice. Consumers Union disclaims responsibility or liability for any loss that may be incurred as a result of the use or application of any information included in **Consumer Reports Best of Health**. Readers should always consult their physicians or other professionals for treatment and advice.

# Contents

# Preface

**Consumer Reports Best of Health** is published by Consumers Union, the nonprofit organization that publishes Consumer Reports on Health, a monthly newsletter on nutrition, fitness, and medical matters, and CONSUMER REPORTS, the monthly magazine best known for test reports, product Ratings, and buying guidance. CONSUMER REPORTS is also a comprehensive source of unbiased advice about products and services, personal finance, health and nutrition, and other consumer concerns. Since 1936, our mission has been to test products, inform the public, and protect consumers. Our income is derived solely from the sale of CONSUMER REPORTS magazine and our other publications and services, and from nonrestrictive, noncommercial contributions, grants, and fees. We buy all the products we test, just as you do. We accept no ads from companies, nor do we let any company use our reports or Ratings for commercial purposes.

# SERVICES FROM CONSUMER REPORTS

**CONSUMER REPORTS.** Published monthly, CONSUMER REPORTS magazine provides impartial information on brand-name products, services, health, and personal finance. To subscribe (13 issues, including the annual buying guide, $26), write to us at our Customer Service Department, P.O. Box 2109, Harlan, Iowa 51593-0298.

**CONSUMER REPORTS ON HEALTH.** Subscription rates: U.S. only: $24 for 1 year, $39 for 2 years. All other countries add $6 per year. (Canadian subscriptions include all taxes, GST registration No. 127047702.) Phone orders and subscription problems: 800-234-2188.

**CONSUMER REPORTS MONEY ADVISER.** Monthly newsletter offering financial advice and money-saving tips. $24 for 1 year (12 issues), $39 for 2 years. To subscribe write us at Money Adviser, P.O. Box 5618, Harlan, Iowa 51593-1118, or call our service line: 800-234-1970.

**CONSUMER REPORTS SPECIAL PUBLICATIONS.** We publish a series of specialty buying guides on cars, computers, and products for the home, as well as books on finance, drugs, and other issues of consumer concern. CONSUMER REPORTS Special Publications are available on newsstands and in bookstores, or through our Web store *(www.Consumer Reports.org/books)*.

**CONSUMER REPORTS ONLINE.** Our Web site, *www.Consumer Reports.org*, offers convenient access to our information and advice. Free areas provide useful listings, shopping guidance, product recalls, and sample reports. Site subscribers pay $4.95 a month or $26 a year ($19 for CONSUMER REPORTS subscribers) for unlimited use of searchable Ratings (including new e-Ratings of e-commerce sites), recommendations, and consumer advice, along with the current issue of CONSUMER REPORTS and participation in message boards.

**AUTOMOTIVE INFORMATION.** Consumer Reports New Car Price Service: Our reports compare sticker price to dealer's invoice. Call 800-933-5555. Consumer Reports Used Car Price Service: Find the market value and reliability data for most 1983 to 1998 cars. Call 800-422-1083.

# Introduction

A popular feature in the **Consumer Reports on Health** newsletters is "On Your Mind," a column in which the editors answer questions from readers on a wide variety of health topics. Most of the contents of *The Best of Health* have been drawn from this source.

*The Best of Health* also includes many "Office Visit" columns, a regular feature in **Consumer Reports on Health,** by Marvin M. Lipman, M.D., Consumers Union's chief medical adviser. These discussions, highly readable and full of practical advice, cover a wide range of health problems. The case histories are taken directly from Dr. Lipman's own medical practice. Irwin D. Mandel, D.D.S., Consumers Union's dental consultant, joins the discussion with an "Office Visit" on 66 and 69. And guest columnist R. Linsy Farris, M.D., M.P.H., weighs in on page 105.

*The Best of Health* is easy to use. Each major topic is listed alphabetically, with specific problems arranged under the appropriate heading. Following many of the main questions and answers are "Office Visit" columns that discuss the same topic from a different angle and in greater detail.

Simply check the table of contents or consult the index to find the subjects that interest you. You're bound to find some questions (and answers) or some health-topic discussions that affect you, a family member, or a friend. Or read the book straight through. Once you get started, *The Best of Health* is hard to put down.

We think you'll find this book enlightening, entertaining, and a valuable source of reliable medical information. All the information has been carefully checked for accuracy and currency.

# Allergies

## DUST-MITE CONTROL

**Q** *Both my wife and I are allergic to dust mites and have tried the recommended step of washing our bedding every two weeks in hot water. However, hot water shrinks and ruins many items like comforters, blankets, and flannel sheets. A product called* De-Mite, *a laundry additive, claims to eliminate dust mites, even in cold water. Does this product really work? Also, do the carpet sprays and powders effectively "neutralize" dust mites and their allergens?*

**A** The active ingredient in *De-Mite*, benzyl benzoate, does indeed effectively kill dust mites when added to laundry detergent in a cool-water wash. A German study found that ordinary detergent with a benzyl benzoate additive eliminated 99.8 percent of dust mites from textiles—compared with a 70.4 percent reduction without the additive—when used with 86° F wash water. Some carpet treatments also use benzyl benzoate, while others contain tannic acid. Both have been shown to neutralize dust-mite allergens for a few months. However, if you have wall-to-wall carpets, your best bet is to completely remove them from the house.

---

## LESS ALLERGENIC FLOWERS

**Q** *Flowers seem to aggravate my allergies. Are certain types less likely to do that?*

**A** Yes. The key is the flowers' aroma, since you're probably reacting to their smell, not their pollen. (Unlike grass pollen and most tree pollens, flower pollens seldom get into the air; they're actually spread mainly by insects and animals rather than wind.) So try to choose relatively low-scent flowers, such as crocuses, daffodils, daisies, certain roses, and tulips.

## ALLERGY SHOTS

**Q** I've had chronic nasal congestion and figured it was due to an allergy. After skin tests confirmed my hunch, my ear-nose- and- throat doctor started giving me desensitization shots. He said I'll need them for the rest of my life. Is that true?

**A** Probably not. Your allergic sensitivity can eventually fade as you age. Allergy shots should be given only as frequently as needed to control symptoms. Typically, that means once a month, perhaps more during allergy season. If symptoms improve, the interval between shots can be increased. Recent evidence has even shown that the benefits of allergy shots may last longer than previously believed.

## ANTIHISTAMINES IN ADVANCE?

**Q** Should antihistamines be taken prior to allergy season, before symptoms develop, in order to build up immunity against the onslaught of allergens?

**A** No. Antihistamines have no such "priming" effect. They help to combat allergic symptoms only when allergens (allergy-inducing substances) are present.

## ALLERGY MEDICATION

**Q** *I suffer from hay-fever types of allergies (sneezing, sinus headache, watery eyes) and have found that taking one* Drixoral *each night helps relieve those symptoms the following day. Should I be concerned that taking this for a long time will cause side effects?*

**A** *Drixoral Cold and Allergy,* an over-the-counter drug that's a long-acting combination of the decongestant pseudo-ephedrine and an antihistamine, has few long-term side effects. Some of the short-term effects, such as sedation, may even lessen with continued use. But by using a fixed-dose combination drug, you may be taking more than what is needed to treat your allergy symptoms. If sneezing and watery eyes are your main problem, an antihistamine alone would usually suffice, and the decongestant ingredient in *Drixoral* would be unnecessary.

---

# Arm, leg, and foot ailments

## NUMB HAND AND ARM

**Q** *I experience recurring numbness during the day or night, especially in two fingers of the right hand. And I often wake up with my entire left arm numb and cold. What's the problem?*

**A** Your favorite sleeping position—like placing your hand under your pillow—could be numbing your left arm by putting pressure on a nerve. If so, feeling should return soon after you wake up and change position. Daytime numbness in your other hand most likely reflects a pinched nerve in your neck. Ask your doctor about being evaluated for disorders such as disk disease or arthritis of the neck, both of which are usually treatable with exercise, drugs, or, as a last resort, surgery.

## COLD HANDS AND FEET

**Q** *My hands and feet are always cold. Does that signal some physical disorder?*

**A** Usually not. Some people have cold extremities for no apparent reason. In others, the coldness stems from anxiety or stress. It's also a side effect of certain drugs, notably beta-blockers and many migraine-fighting drugs. However, if your fingers or toes temporarily turn white, the coldness is probably caused by Raynaud's disease, a common condition that impairs circulation to the extremities. Severe cases can lead to fingertip ulceration. And Raynaud's occasionally signals a more serious disease such as scleroderma or lupus. Treatment includes stopping smoking, keeping the hands and feet warm, and if necessary, taking blood-vessel-dilating ACE inhibitors or calcium-channel blockers.

## CORN-REMOVAL CONCERNS

**Q** *A podiatrist told me that the acid in a medicated corn-removal pad can eat away not only the corn but also healthy skin, possibly causing infection. Is that true?*

**A** Yes. That's why the medicated pads should be small enough that they touch only the corn—a buildup of thick, hardened skin—not the surrounding area. Don't wear them longer than 48 hours, and check periodically to make sure the pad hasn't shifted off the corn. Never use pads on skin that is irritated or infected, and avoid them if you have diabetes or poor circulation, both of which increase the chance of irritation and infection. If you have none of those conditions and want an alternative to pads, try gently rubbing the corn with a callus file or pumice stone, available at drugstores, or even with a rough towel. Pharmacies also sell nonmedicated cushions, gel toe sleeves, and lambswool padding, which can ease discomfort when you walk. Wearing properly fitted shoes and having foot deformities treated can keep corns from developing or returning.

## STUB OUT TOENAIL FUNGUS?

**Q** *Is there any cure for the fungus that is deforming my toenails?*

**A** Yes—but the cure could be worse than the infection, which may not require treatment at all. The oral drugs itraconazole *(Sporanox)* and terbinafine *(Lamisil)* will usually eradicate the fungus. But liver damage is a rare side effect of both drugs, and itraconazole has caused a few cases of heart failure. Alternatively, your doctor could prescribe another antifungal, fluconazole *(Diflucan)*, which hasn't been approved by the Food and Drug Administration for treating toenails, but appears to be effective and somewhat safer than the other two. All three drugs can cause other, milder side effects and may interact with several medications. And they're expensive. Fortunately, while the fungus thickens, roughens, and discolors the nails, it usually causes no discomfort. And while the untreated infection almost always persists, it rarely spreads or gets worse. So it's generally best to forgo treatment if you can live with the condition.

## IS KNEE SURGERY NECESSARY?

**Q** *I'm an avid hiker and my knee has begun to bother me slightly, though not enough to keep me from hiking. After a test showed a small tear in the meniscus of my knee, a surgeon recommended arthroscopic surgery to prevent it from getting worse. Is that surgery necessary?*

**A** Probably, if the tear in the meniscus, the knee's shock-absorbing cartilage, doesn't heal on its own. To facilitate healing, avoid hiking for six to eight weeks; meanwhile, treat your knee with an anti-inflammatory drug such as ibuprofen *(Advil, Motrin)*. If that doesn't ease the discomfort, it's generally better not to wait for the pain and the tear to get worse before turning to surgery. Studies have found that repairing such tears when they're still small leads to better postsurgical recovery and lowers the risk of further joint problems or osteoarthritis. As operations go, arthroscopic knee surgery, performed with miniature instruments inserted through very small incisions, is fairly routine. It has a very low risk of complications and a high likelihood of success, a short recovery time, and relatively little postoperative pain.

## BONE SPURS

**Q** *My foot doctor has advised surgery for painful bone spurs on the top of my feet. But I can't afford to stay off my feet for eight weeks. Would medication, laser treatment, or anything else relieve the pain?*

**A** Bone spurs, an overgrowth of bone at or near joints (usually those of the big toe), don't cause pain; shoe pressure on the spurs does. Try wearing roomier shoes, stretch shoes, or extra-depth orthopedic shoes. Putting pads inside your regular shoes may help, so long as the pads don't put more pressure on the spurs. Aspirin or ibuprofen may relieve the pain temporarily, but that's not a long-term solution. Sometimes an injection of a long-acting corticosteroid *(Depo-Medrol, Hydrocortone)* can provide relief for months.

If those simple measures aren't sufficient, surgery to file down the protuberances may indeed be your best bet. Recovery from surgery rarely takes eight weeks, however. Most people can resume sedentary activities, such as desk work, within a few days and light walking without crutches or a cane in three or four weeks. So far, laser treatment for bone spurs seems to offer no advantage over traditional surgery.

## FEET ON FIRE

**Q** *I have a severe burning feeling on the soles of both feet. My circulation is normal, and soaking and applying powders haven't helped. Could this be a symptom of a serious ailment?*

**A** A burning sensation on the soles of your feet can arise from any number of causes, from ill-fitting shoes to diabetes. The most serious cause is peripheral neuropathy—damage to the leg nerves—often from diabetes or alcoholism and less commonly from vitamin deficiencies or lead poisoning. A rare disorder called erythromelalgia increases blood flow to the hands and feet and can also produce a searing sensation.

Some people experience fiery feet because they're sensitive to a chemical in the inner lining of their shoes (particularly some types of athletic shoes). Try changing your footgear to see if the problem subsides. If not, see your physician to rule out medical causes.

## TREATING SWOLLEN LEGS

**Q** I've had lymphedema in both legs for 12 years, and my ability to walk has steadily worsened. My doctor's only recommendation is an extremity pump to pressurize a sleeve that covers each leg. Are there any other treatments?

**A** Lymphedema is swelling of an arm or leg due to obstruction of the flow of lymph, a milky-looking body fluid. Leg swelling from lymphedema can be treated in several ways, but all treatments lose effectiveness over time. The "lymph pump" you describe can provide temporary relief early on, when fluid accumulation is less severe. The primary treatment for lymphedema remains the use of good elastic stockings. Various surgical procedures have been tried, generally with little lasting benefit.

---

## WATERLOGGED LEGS

**Q** I am a 75-year-old woman. Last year my feet and legs became so swollen that I couldn't get into my shoes. My doctor said I had "water retention" and gave me a seven-day supply of Maxzide [triamterene and hydrochlorothiazide], which eventually relieved the swelling. What causes water retention, and how can I avoid it?

**A** There are several reasons for leg swelling. One of the most common is varicose veins, in which damage to valves in the large veins of the legs hinders the return of blood to the heart. Blood plasma, which is mostly water, pools in nearby tissue, causing swelling of the legs and feet. Excess dietary salt, sitting or standing for long periods, and hot weather can aggravate the swelling. Exercise such as walking or cycling helps. So does resting with your legs elevated. Water retention can also be caused by more serious problems, such as heart, liver, and kidney disorders. A medical checkup to rule those out would be wise.

---

## ✚ *Office* Visit

# NUMB TOES, TINGLING FINGERS

"It's as if I were walking on pillows," said a 72-year-old retired college professor when he came to me recently complaining that both of his feet felt numb. He turned out to be deficient in vitamin B12, which can cause a common condition called peripheral neuropathy—loss of sensation, followed by muscle weakness and atrophy, in the affected extremity. Vitamin B12 supplementation quickly resolved his numbness.

Neuropathy can have a number of causes. Probably the most common is mechanical pressure on a nerve. Under compression, the first nerve fibers to lose function are the ones that conduct sensation. As the sensory fibers "go to sleep," the first signal perceived is the familiar "pins-and-needles" tingling sensation.

### PRESSURE POINTS

Certain nerves are especially vulnerable to compression. People who sleep curled up with one hand tucked under their head put pressure on the median nerve as it passes through the wrist's carpal tunnel. The resultant tingling sensation will usually awaken the person long enough to shake the hand and restore normal feeling.

But some compression neuropathies can produce longer-lasting damage. Compression of the radial nerve causes "Saturday night palsy"—so-called because Saturday used to be the weekly payday for army recruits. After an evening of serious drinking, soldiers would fall asleep at the bar with their head resting on the backs of their wrist. Radial-nerve palsy was the result, and recovery sometimes took months.

Nearly everyone has banged his or her "funny bone," producing tingling in the pinky and half of the ring finger. This isn't a bone at all, but rather the ulnar nerve, which lies close to the skin at the elbow. Ulnar neuropathy is seen most often in people who continually lean on their elbows. In severe cases it can temporarily paralyze the affected fingers.

Another peripheral nerve, the peroneal nerve, runs perilously close to the skin just below the outside of the knee, where it can be compressed by prolonged crossing of the legs while sitting. That can cause tingling along the outside of the lower leg and also, occasionally, "foot drop"—the inability to raise the foot. During recovery, which can be slow, a foot brace may be needed to help with walking.

## INTERNAL PRESSURE

Nerves can also be compressed near their roots as they emerge from the spinal cord. Pressure can come from arthritic bone spurs, protruding disks, disk fragments, or overgrowth of bone surrounding the hole through which the nerve exits (spinal stenosis).

The most common spinal compression neuropathy, sciatica, probably has better name recognition than some members of the Supreme Court. Pressure on the long sciatic nerve produces a burning ache that radiates from the buttock down the back of the thigh, into the lower leg and foot. Leg weakness can occur because of muscle atrophy.

Some diseases and conditions, such as the professor's vitamin B12 deficiency, affect peripheral nerves directly. Others in this category include diabetes, rheumatoid arthritis, lupus, thiamin deficiency, and kidney failure. Sometimes neuropathies can result from too much vitamin B6, certain types of cancer chemotherapy, or chronic alcoholism.

## DIAGNOSIS AND TREATMENT

Anyone who has persistent numbness, tingling, or weakness in an extremity should get a careful history and physical examination, including tests of reflexes, sensation, and muscle strength. Nerve-conduction studies can help determine how bad the problem is and localize the site of a compression neuropathy. CT scans and magnetic resonance imaging may also be necessary.

If the source of pressure is external, getting rid of it is generally enough to correct mild, newly developed compression neuropathies. But more severe or long-standing cases often require more aggressive treatment. The initial prescription is usually an anti-inflammatory medication such as ibuprofen *(Advil)*, often followed by some combination of splinting, physiotherapy, corticosteroid injections, and occupational therapy. Invasive measures, such as spinal surgery, are only a last resort.

Treatment of neuropathies caused by disease varies according to the cause. There is, unfortunately, no good treatment for diabetic neuropathy, the most common disease-related form. People with this condition must learn to be vigilant about foot and hand hygiene and to inspect their extremities regularly for small cuts and bruises.

## Arthritis, joint, and muscle disorders

### DOES FOOD AGGRAVATE ARTHRITIS?

**Q** *A friend recently stopped drinking orange juice because she heard that citrus fruits could aggravate her arthritis. Is that a valid concern?*

**A** Though some people who have arthritis—mainly rheumatoid—claim they experience adverse reactions to one food or another, such associations are uncommon. In one of the few reliable studies, 52 of the 159 participants claimed that food aggravated their arthritis. But actual tests were unable to confirm a single instance. A subsequent review of the available evidence concluded that food-induced flare-ups were rare or at most occasional. If your friend believes she has such a food reaction, she should consult a rheumatologist.

### HEAT OR COLD FOR ARTHRITIS?

**Q** *Is it better to treat arthritis symptoms with heat or cold?*

**A** That depends on the symptoms. Cold reduces inflammation and swelling and relieves pain better than heat (though alternating between cold and heat provides greater relief for some people). But cold may increase joint stiffness. Heat relaxes muscles and tendons and promotes circulation, so it's the best choice for boosting the mobility of stiff joints. Finally, heat and cold can each help tame muscle spasms.

Whichever approach you choose, follow these precautions:

• Apply heat or cold for only 15 to 20 minutes at a time, letting the skin return to normal temperature before reapplying.

• Place a cloth or towel between your skin and the heating or cooling device.

• Stop immediately if your skin blisters or turns either dark red or spotty red and white.

Don't use heat or cold on damaged skin. And don't use them at all if you suffer from poor circulation, nerve damage, or a condition that may cause either of those problems, such as diabetes, Raynaud's disease, or vasculitis.

## MUSCLE CRAMPS

**Q** *As I've grown older, I've started getting muscle cramps. What can I do about them?*

**A** For most cramps, stretch. If a spasm strikes the calf (by far the most common cramp site), pull the front of the foot up toward the knee. Since cramps usually result from muscle fatigue, you may be able to prevent such spasms by gently stretching before you exercise your calves. Stand a few feet from a wall, brace yourself against the wall with your hands, and lean forward, keeping your heels on the ground until you feel a pull in your calves. This maneuver before bedtime can also help prevent unexplained nighttime spasms.

If the cause isn't muscle fatigue, your physician may find other, possibly treatable causes. These can include circulatory problems, hyperventilation, an underactive thyroid, and low blood levels of calcium or (rarely) magnesium.

## BURSITIS OF THE HIP

**Q** *How common is bursitis of the hip, and what can be done about it? I had my first siege 10 months ago, and although Feldene helped a lot, the bursitis has not disappeared entirely.*

**A** Although bursitis most often affects the shoulder, bursitis of the hip is also quite common. Knees and elbows are also vulnerable. At all those joints, tiny sacs called bursae cover the area where the tendon attaches to the bone. When a bursa becomes inflamed, often because of injury or overuse, the joint aches. Standard treatment consists of rest and oral anti-inflammatory medication such as naproxen *(Aleve, Naprosyn)*. Sometimes injections of a corticosteroid drug directly into the bursa can be helpful. The inflammation and pain usually pass with time but can recur. In rare instances, surgery may be necessary.

## FIBROMYALGIA: WHAT DOES IT MEAN?

**Q** *I have been diagnosed as having fibromyalgia, which comes and goes. I would appreciate an explanation of what it is and whether it is curable or controllable.*

**A** Fibromyalgia, also known as fibrositis or fibromyositis, refers to a disorder of unknown cause that is characterized by recurrent pain in the joints, muscles, or tendons. Often small, specific areas called "trigger points" are tender to the touch. Physical strain and cold or damp weather can make the disorder worse. Frequently, the pain is associated with other symptoms, such as insomnia, fatigue, or anxiety. Laboratory tests are usually normal. There are several treatments: physical therapy, warm or cold compresses, anti-inflammatory medication, and sometimes an anesthetic or cortisone injected directly into the trigger points. The symptoms can wax and wane over many years.

## GOUT AND THE DIET

**Q** *In addition to taking medication for gout, I also avoid foods high in purine—such as animal organs, herring, mushrooms, sardines, and spinach. I've been told my list of purine-containing foods is incomplete. What others should I avoid?*

**A** Many other foods contain purines, notably anchovies, goose, mussels, scallops, yeast, and meat derivatives such as soup stock and gravy. But avoiding purine-containing foods may not be as necessary as it was once thought to be.

Gout is a heritable disease marked by an excess of uric acid in the blood. Severe dietary restriction for people with gout can indeed decrease blood levels of uric acid somewhat. However, today's medications, especially allopurinol *(Lopurin, Zyloprim),* can do the job much better. So moderation in diet rather than avoidance of certain foods is sufficient for most people with gout.

Alcohol, however, is one dietary item that should be restricted, since it may trigger an acute attack of gout.

## RUB IT IN

**Q** *What is it about* BenGay *that helps relieve the pain of arthritis?*

**A** *BenGay,* like other muscle-ache and arthritis rubs, provides relief by acting as a counterirritant. It produces a mild local inflammation that crowds out pain messages from nearby muscles and joints. Arthritis rubs also create heat by increasing blood flow to the area; because of the risk of a burn, they should never be used together with a heating pad.

---

## ✚ *Office* Visit

# A RED, HOT PAINFUL KNEE

"I DON'T RECALL INJURING IT," said the 54-year-old grade-school teacher. "It began aching last night, and this morning it was already swollen, warm to the touch, and bright red. And it hurts so much that I can hardly walk on it." A glance at her left knee confirmed her classic description of acute monoarticular (one-joint) arthritis.

An inflamed knee is hardly a rare condition, but it's a symptom, not a disease—and it can have many causes. So the next step was to do some diagnostic sleuthing.

My patient hadn't injured her knee, which can cause bleeding into the joint and inflammation. Her history gave no reason to suspect infectious arthritis. And the fact that this office visit was taking place in January in New York state greatly reduced the possibility of Lyme disease.

I looked carefully for swelling in her knuckles and finger joints and found no clues to suggest her arthritis was caused by rheumatoid disease.

### FINDING THE CAUSE

Cutting to the chase, I asked a rheumatologist colleague to remove some fluid from my patient's knee. Examining the fluid under a microscope, the rheumatologist identified sodium urate crystals—the giveaway clue to the diagnosis: gout. A later test showed she had an elevated blood uric-acid level.

Gout acquired its indelible image as "a complaint as arises from too much ease and comfort," from Charles Dickens' 1836 novel, "The Pickwick Papers." While dietary excesses and exuberant use of alcohol can indeed trigger attacks of gout, that 19th-century stereotype was not applicable to my slim, teetotaling patient.

Gout, which affects men much more commonly than women, usually arises from an inborn error of metabolism that results in an excess of uric acid in the blood. But anything that elevates blood uric acid can cause gout, including the use of diuretics such as furosemide *(Lasix)*, alcohol, leukemia and other bone-marrow malignancies, and—for reasons we don't fully understand—trauma and surgery.

An accumulation of uric-acid crystals in the joints can irritate certain cells, which then release chemicals that can cause inflammation and acute, often unbearable, pain. With repeated attacks in the same joint, uric-acid deposits called tophi can disfigure the joint and impair mobility and function.

In addition, when excess uric acid is excreted in the urine, it can result in formation of painful uric-acid kidney stones and cause infection and obstruction of urine flow. Those stones can be reduced in size and sometimes even dissolved by taking sodium bicarbonate orally to alkalinize the urine.

## TREATING GOUT

The treatment of acute gout is relatively simple. Adequate doses of over-the-counter nonsteroidal anti-inflammatory drugs (NSAIDs) such as ibuprofen *(Advil, Motrin)* or naproxen *(Aleve)* can work near-miraculous results within 24 hours but should be continued for about five days. Colchicine, a medication that dates back to ancient China, is still used by many for the treatment of acute gout. However, the resultant diarrhea can be more disabling than the painful joint.

When acute attacks of gout recur, thought has to be given to prevention. Because uric acid is derived from purines, chemicals produced during the metabolism of protein, the traditional preventive treatment has been to cut back on purine-rich protein, especially organ meats.

Since the advent in the early 1980s of a medication called allopurinol *(Zyloprim)*, which limits the formation of uric acid, stringent adherence to a low-purine diet is no longer necessary. Allopurinol effectively prevents both acute gout attacks and the formation of uric-acid kidney stones. Colchicine, in lower doses that don't cause diarrhea, can also be used to prevent attacks. Probenecid, another medication, which increases urinary excretion of uric acid, is useful for those allergic to allopurinol but not in those predisposed to kidney stones.

As for our schoolteacher, after three days on full anti-inflammatory doses of ibuprofen, her knee was as good as new. I put her on colchicine twice daily as a preventive for the following six weeks. That was a year and a half ago. So far—so good.

# Asthma and lung problems

## ASTHMA AND GAS STOVES

**Q** *I understand that using a wood-burning fireplace or stove can aggravate asthma and allergies. Is that also true of such appliances that use gas logs?*

**A** Like woodstoves, all gas-burning appliances emit several invisible combustion byproducts, such as carbon monoxide and nitrous oxides, some of which can irritate the lungs. A recent study of 539 adults with asthma found that those who used gas stoves daily were twice as likely to suffer severe asthma attacks as those who never used such appliances. Since the offending pollutants are too small to be filtered out of the air, the only way to reduce or eliminate them is to improve the ventilation or give up the gas.

## BLOOD CLOTS IN THE LUNG

**Q** *Four weeks after a hysterectomy, my 62-year-old mother died suddenly due to pulmonary emboli, or blood clots in her lung. Should my sisters and I worry that this could happen to us after surgery?*

**A** That depends. Susceptibility to pulmonary embolism, which generally develops only after surgery or prolonged bed rest, is not inherited directly. However, two risk factors for the condition—obesity and severe varicose veins—do run in families. Other risk factors include heart failure, certain cancers, a history of phlebitis (inflamed veins), and long rides in trains and airplanes. People predisposed to pulmonary embolism may receive anticlotting medication after they've undergone abdominal, pelvic, or certain orthopedic operations—or if they'll be bed-ridden for a long time or taking a long flight.

## GOOD MOVES FOR ASTHMATICS

**Q** *I'm considering a change of climate to help relieve my asthma. I've heard that the dry air of the desert Southwest is beneficial, but also that salty sea air can help. Can you clear up this contradiction?*

**A** The best locale for asthma sufferers is one that's free of pollutants, airborne allergens, and frigid weather. Traditionally, asthmatics migrated to Arizona for its warm, dry climate, although the benefit came primarily from cleaner air and lower pollen counts. As Arizona cities have grown, however, the environment there has become less favorable for asthmatics. Sea air has no effect on asthma.

## CHEST CONGESTION

**Q** *I often have congestion in my nose, ears, and chest. What over-the-counter drugs would you recommend to loosen this congestion in my chest so I can cough it up and spit it out?*

**A** The only FDA-approved expectorant for loosening phlegm is guaifenesin. It's found in *Breonesin* tablets, plain *Robitussin* syrup, *Scot-Tussin* syrup, and other over-the-counter products.However, an expectorant doesn't address the underlying problem and therefore should be used only occasionally. You may have a chronic problem in your sinuses or bronchial airways. You should be evaluated by a physician for allergies or any other problem that might cause recurrent congestion.

## ✚ *Office* **Visit**

# A DANGEROUS, OFTEN OVERLOOKED PROBLEM

LAST SUMMER A 68-YEAR-OLD WOMAN came to my office complaining of severe pain in the right side of her midback. The same complaint had taken her to the hospital emergency room the night before, where the doctor sent her home on pain medication with a diagnosis of "back sprain."

What my patient hadn't mentioned to the ER doctor (and what he had failed to ask) was that the pain intensified every time she took a deep breath, and that 10 days before, she had undergone minor pelvic surgery.

The chest X-ray I ordered for her was normal, but a nuclear lung scan showed a high probability of a blood clot. I sent her straight to the hospital with a diagnosis of pulmonary embolism, which, if left untreated, could have resulted in a life-threatening recurrence.

## AN UNDERDIAGNOSED PROBLEM

There aren't many medical conditions that elude diagnosis as often as pulmonary embolism. It kills about 50,000 people annually. Most fatal cases are not recognized until after death. Emboli are substances that not only block an artery, but have traveled to the site of blockage from a distant area. Fat globules can act as emboli after a limb fracture or liposuction, amniotic fluid during the active-labor stage of childbirth, and air during neurosurgery. However, most emboli are blood clots. The lungs are the primary target, and the deep veins of the legs are by far the most common origin. Sometimes, as in my patient, veins in the pelvis (or abdomen) can be the source, especially after surgery in those areas.

Blood clots in the large leg veins, known as deep-vein thromboses, rarely develop in healthy people without good reason. Groups at risk include those who have already had the condition and the following:

• Women who are pregnant, and those who take oral contraceptives, postmenopausal estrogens, the breast-cancer drug tamoxifen *(Nolvadex)*, and the antiosteoporosis medication raloxifene *(Evista)*.

• People who have had pelvic, abdominal, hip, or knee surgery, or trauma to a leg, within the past 10 days.

• People with congestive heart failure, whose risk is especially high during periods of inactivity, such as prolonged bed rest or a long airplane ride.

## RECOGNIZING THROMBOSIS

The symptoms of deep-vein thrombosis can range from nonexistent to severe pain and swelling of the calf or thigh. Those with symptoms are actually the lucky ones, because, left untreated, 50 to 60 percent of people whose blood clot elongates to six inches or more and extends from the calf into the deep thigh veins will develop pulmonary embolism. Conversely, about 70 percent of people with pulmonary embolism will turn out to have deep-vein thrombosis (usually diagnosed by ultrasound) in a leg.

Pulmonary embolism is difficult to diagnose because its symptoms, as in my patient, can mislead physicians. The classic symptoms—shortness of breath, pain on breathing, cough, and bloody sputum—don't often occur together and, even when they do, can be caused by plenty of other diseases.

The gold standard for the diagnosis of pulmonary embolism is the pulmonary angiogram, an invasive procedure in which a catheter is inserted in the groin and snaked up through the right side of the heart and into the pulmonary artery. Dye is injected and any obstruction to the flow of blood within the lungs can be seen. Though relatively safe, the test is cumbersome and requires the presence of a radiologist, who may not be available. For those reasons it winds up being used in only about 1 case in 10. More commonly used but less specific tests are CT scans, magnetic resonance imaging, and the nuclear lung scan used in my patient.

In my patient's case, the combination of symptoms, test results, and the history of a recent pelvic operation led me to the diagnosis of pulmonary embolism. She stayed in the hospital for five days of treatment with intravenous heparin, a potent blood thinner. Since her discharge four months ago, she has continued to take warfarin *(Coumadin),* a blood-thinning medication, and has remained well. After two more months, her course of treatment will be ended.

## WHEN TO WORRY

If you're predisposed to deep-vein thrombosis because of any of the factors mentioned above, call your doctor immediately if you experience any of the following symptoms:

- Acute shortness of breath.
- Sudden chest pain when you take a deep breath.
- Cough that comes on abruptly in the absence of a respiratory infection.
- Bloody sputum.
- Leg or calf pain.

## Back pain

### DISK DECISION

**Q** *Because of a herniated disk, I've been suffering from lower-back pain that radiates to my leg. Is surgery usually necessary, or could other treatment relieve the pain?*

**A** Conservative treatment, including physical therapy and anti-inflammatory drugs, is often successful in relieving pain from a herniated, or "slipped," disk. Unless the pain or numbness is severe or nerve function is impaired to the point of weakness of your leg muscles, you should try those alternatives for two to three months before resorting to more invasive techniques such as local cortisone injections or surgery.

### PUSH-UPS AND BAD BACKS

**Q** *I've read that anyone with a "bad back" should not do push-ups. I've never experienced any back problems that I could attribute to push-ups, but now I am concerned. Please elaborate.*

**A** Done correctly, push-ups shouldn't harm your back at all. The key is to keep your upper body straight as you push up, whether pivoting from your toes (the classic position) or from your knees (the "modified" push-up). If you arch your back, you'll strain it. That's a common mistake, so people who have had back problems should probably skip push-ups.

## MIACALCIN AND BACKACHE

**Q** *I had been taking* Miacalcin *for osteoporosis for two to three months when a previously mild backache became very painful and my fatigue seemed to increase. The pharmacist said that both these symptoms could be due to* Miacalcin. *What is it about* Miacalcin *that causes these side effects?*

**A** The manufacturer of *Miacalcin Nasal Spray* (calcitonin) reports that about 5 percent of people taking the nasal spray complain of backache. Fewer than 3 percent report fatigue. It's not clear why the drug, a synthetic version of a hormone made by cells within the thyroid, causes these problems. If you continue to have trouble, ask your doctor about other medications for osteoporosis, such as alendronate *(Fosamax)* and risedronate *(Actonel)*.

## Bladder and urinary problems

## LONG-TERM DIURETICS

**Q** *I take a diuretic medication every day. Does the drug lose its effectiveness or cause any harm when taken for many years?*

**A** No. Diuretics (drugs that increase urine output) are an effective long-term therapy for hypertension and other disorders. Long-term use doesn't cause harm, although it can result in a low blood-potassium level, which can damage the kidneys.

## RESTLESS NIGHTS

**Q** *For the past couple of years, an aching fullness in my bladder has prompted me to get up as many as three to four
times a night to urinate. I do not experience the same problem
during the day. I am 25 years old, female, and otherwise in good
health. Do I need to see a doctor?*

**A** Not necessarily. First, try drinking less fluid with dinner and
during the evening. In particular, refrain from alcohol and caffeine which are diuretics. But if those simple measures don't work,
see your doctor. Your "nocturia" could be due to an enlarged pelvic
structure pressing on the bladder when you lie down, the nighttime
release of daytime water retention, or a kidney disorder.

---

## INTERSTITIAL CYSTITIS

**Q** *What can you tell me about interstitial cystitis? I know it re-
sembles a urinary-tract infection, but it's not an infection.*

**A** You're right. Interstitial cystitis is a bladder inflammation,
but infection is not to blame. Like a urinary-tract infection,
the disease can provoke frequent, urgent urination. Unlike an infection, it often causes pain that is actually relieved by urination.
   No one knows what causes interstitial cystitis, and diagnosis
can be difficult. There is no cure, so treatment focuses on symptoms. Many approaches have been tried, including distending the
bladder with fluid; infusing the bladder with a chemical called
DMSO *(Rimso-50)*; and giving oral medications such as pentosan
*(Elmiron)*, the antidepressant amitriptyline *(Elavil)*, and various
muscle relaxants for the bladder. None has worked consistently.
   In one study, patients who didn't have severe pain gradually

stretched their bladder by resisting the urge to urinate frequently. Each month they increased the interval between trips to the bathroom by 15 to 30 minutes. After three months, 15 of the 21 patients reported at least a 50 percent reduction in the urgency and frequency of urination.

Since the disorder often defies medical therapy, patients have formed a self-help group: The Interstitial Cystitis Association (800 HELP-ICA or 301 610-5300; *www.ichelp.com*).

## CANCEROUS BLADDER POLYPS

**Q** *My urologist found bladder polyps when he did a cystoscopy on me. After removing them, he said they were cancerous but "low-grade, superficial, and noninvasive." What causes malignant bladder polyps?*

**A** Occasionally, a specific carcinogen can be pinpointed as the cause of malignant polyps. The main culprits are cigarette smoking and occupational exposure to aromatic amines, compounds used in many manufacturing and chemical processes. More recently, hair dyes have been implicated. In most cases, however, there's no identifiable cause.

Malignant bladder polyps range from slow-growing, noninvasive tumors to aggressive cancers that rapidly invade the bladder wall. Bladder polyps can also turn out to be benign. In either case, the most effective treatment is removal of the polyps through a cystoscope, a lighted tube inserted into the bladder. After removal of a malignant polyp, the bladder should be reinspected cystoscopically every three to six months for several years.

# Blood pressure

## BALANCING POTASSIUM NEEDS

*I have read that it's important to have 4,000 to 5,000 mil-ligrams of potassium daily, mainly to keep blood pressure down. We regularly eat bananas and have a daily glass of orange juice, but those foods total only about 800 milligrams. My husband and I are in our mid-60s, and he is taking Prinivil for high blood pressure (mine is low). Should we strive to meet that potassium guideline?*

Potassium has been shown to modestly reduce blood pressure, but that doesn't mean that more is better for everyone. Your husband, for instance, shouldn't increase his potassium intake as long as he is taking lisinopril *(Prinivil)*. Like all the blood-pressure drugs known as ACE inhibitors, lisinopril has a tendency to cause the kidneys to retain potassium. As for yourself, you can easily get all the potassium you need through a diet that contains plenty of fruits, vegetables, and dairy products. Orange juice (503 milligrams per cup) and bananas (451 milligrams each) are just a start. A single baked potato with skin contains 844 milligrams; a half-cup of cooked spinach, 420 milligrams; a cup of low-fat plain yogurt, 531 milligrams.

## THE OTHER HYPERTENSION

*What would cause an increase in a 70-year-old's systolic, or upper, blood-pressure reading while the diastolic pressure remains normal? How serious a problem is this?*

**A** The stiffening of the arteries that typically occurs with advancing age can cause systolic blood pressure (the pressure in the arteries when the heart contracts) to rise above normal without affecting diastolic pressure (the pressure between contractions). An overactive thyroid or anemia can often produce the same effect. Temporary systolic blood-pressure hikes may result from exercise, stress, or excitement.

Until recently, doctors paid little attention to systolic blood pressure. But recent studies have clearly shown that for middle-aged and older people, any increase in systolic blood pressure over 140 mm Hg definitely needs to be controlled.

## LOW BLOOD PRESSURE

**Q** *Recently I tried to donate blood for the first time and was turned away because my blood pressure was too low (80 over 60 that morning). I'm 52 years old and, as far as I know, in good health. I eat a balanced diet and exercise almost every day. But my blood pressure is usually only about 100 over 70. Should I be worried about that low level?*

**A** On the contrary, you should ask for a discount on your life insurance premium! If you feel healthy, having a relatively low blood pressure like yours is good for the cardiovascular system, since it puts less stress on the blood vessels. If you were not in such good health, low blood pressure could indicate a disorder such as coronary heart disease or low blood volume due to blood loss. The only reason why low pressure would disqualify you as a donor is that the additional lowering due to losing a pint of blood could conceivably cause a fainting spell.

## YO-YO BLOOD PRESSURE

**Q** *My blood pressure bounces up and down from day to day, ranging from as high as 180/98 to as low as 107/61. I've been taking blood-pressure medication for years, but this fluctuation is relatively new, and nothing seems to help. Can you offer any suggestions?*

**A** Ask your doctor about taking a 24-hour urine test to screen for an adrenaline-producing tumor called a pheochromocytoma. That treatable condition can cause wildly fluctuating blood pressure. A more common cause is nerve inflammation due to diabetes.

## HEAT AND BLOOD PRESSURE

**Q** *Does using a* Jacuzzi *or* sauna *elevate blood pressure in people who already have hypertension?*

**A** No. In fact, high ambient temperature typically causes blood pressure to drop as blood vessels dilate in order to keep body temperature constant. That drop in blood pressure can cause you to faint, especially if you're already taking antihypertensive medication.

# Bone health

## WHEN TO TAKE BONE-BUILDING DRUGS

**Q** *I'm a healthy 72-year-old woman who exercises frequently. I don't have osteoporosis, but my doctor says that because my mother had the disease, I should take a bone-building drug like alendronate (Fosamax), raloxifene (Evista), or risedronate (Actonel). Is that good advice?*

**A** Not unless your skeleton shows signs of deterioration. If you don't have osteoporosis (rapidly thinning bones), those effective but often overprescribed drugs are generally needed only when bone-density testing reveals mildly thinning bones, and follow-up tests a year or two later show continued thinning. To help fortify your skeleton without drugs, keep exercising regularly and get enough bone-bolstering vitamin D and calcium. (For people over age 65, that's 600 to 800 International Units of D and 1,500 milligrams of calcium a day.)

## TEA AND CALCIUM ABSORPTION

**Q** *I'm an avid tea drinker who's at risk for developing osteoporosis. I take calcium pills, but I've heard tea is high in oxalate, which blocks calcium absorption. Should I up my calcium dosage?*

**A** Probably not. Oxalate, a naturally occurring chemical in many foods, can significantly reduce the body's calcium absorption—but only from the same food, such as spinach and rhubarb, that contains the oxalate. There is no calcium in tea.

And tea's oxalate won't significantly affect the absorption of calcium from supplements or other beverages or foods, even if they're consumed at the same time. In fact, two recent studies found that tea drinkers had stronger bones than nondrinkers, possibly because of the protective effects of flavonoids and fluoride in tea. Although calcium and oxalates can combine to form kidney stones, that condition tends to occur only if you consume lots of oxalate and not enough calcium. And tea may help block stone development in other ways.

## HEIGHT LOSS

**Q** *I'm a 93-year-old, physically active and perfectly healthy woman. But I'm 4 inches shorter than I used to be. Is it normal to shrink with age?*

**A** Yes. After age 40 or so, the disks separating the vertebrae in the spine start to shrink; the back muscles weaken, which may allow posture to slump; and bone mass can decline by as much as 8 percent per decade in women, 3 percent in men. On average, people lose about 3 inches in height by their mid-80s or 90s. (Osteoporosis, or severe bone thinning can drastically reduce height as well, by causing the vertebrae to fracture and collapse.)

## TORTUROUS TAILBONE

**Q** *I've been suffering from coccydynia, or painful tailbone, for over a year. It started suddenly, for no apparent reason, and it makes sitting very painful. I've seen several doctors, but none has helped. Do you have any suggestions?*

**A** First, make sure your doctors have checked for rare tumors and infections in the lower back that can trigger similar symptoms. More often, the problem stems from sprained tailbone ligaments. While that's usually caused by a fall or by difficult delivery of a child, the physical stress of sitting can eventually cause similar damage if you're overweight. If not, the pain may stem from an otherwise benign bone growth on the end of the tailbone. Mild pain can usually be soothed by taking anti-inflammatory drugs such as aspirin or ibuprofen *(Advil, Motrin)*, sitting erect, or sitting on a donut-shaped pillow. But severe pain like yours will probably require stronger treatment. A combination of massage (preceded by a local-anesthetic injection) plus corticosteroid injections usually pacifies the pain. If all else fails and you can't live with the pain, you might consider removal of the entire tailbone, though the procedure is still fairly controversial, and full recovery can take up to a year.

## WHEN TO GET BONES TESTED

**Q** *I'm a 65-year-old woman who takes calcium supplements and raloxifene* (Evista) *to treat osteoporosis. How often should I have a bone-density test?*

**A** For women who already have osteoporosis, doctors have long used periodic bone-density testing to check how well treatment is working. Since raloxifene appears to increase bone density by about 1 percent per year, you don't need to take the test more than once every two years. But such testing is not just for people who already have osteoporosis. Our medical consultants recommend it for detecting the disease in all women age 65 or older, provided they would consider treatment if the test proved positive. Moreover, postmenopausal women under 65

and men over 65 should consider getting tested if mild trauma
has caused a bone fracture or if they have one or more risk factors for osteoporosis. Risk factors include a family history of
early menopause or osteoporosis, excessive drinking or smoking,
insufficient dietary calcium, sedentary lifestyle, and, to a lesser extent, being thin and white.

## TUMS FOR THE BONES

**Q** *My doctor told me to take* Tums, *which is calcium carbonate, as an inexpensive alternative to calcium pills. However,
the bottle warns against taking the maximum dose for more than
two weeks. Is it safe to take* Tums *indefinitely?*

**A** Yes, if you're just taking the modest dose needed as a supplement. The warning on the *Tums* bottle refers to its use as
an antacid: Prolonged need for antacids should be evaluated by a
doctor. Moreover, large amounts of supplemental calcium—such
as the maximum dosage of 16 tablets a day for indigestion—can
cause constipation, abdominal pain, and kidney stones if taken
over a long period.

# Cardiovascular disorders

## RAPID HEARTBEAT

**Q** *My mother-in-law recently experienced a racing heart, about 130 beats per minute, throughout the night. Could that be serious?*

**A** Possibly, depending on the cause. It may have been a response to caffeine or pseudoephedrine *(Sudafed)* taken too close to bedtime. But it could also stem from abnormalities of the nerve pathways that trigger the rhythmic contractions of the heart. The most common abnormalities involve the heart's upper chambers, or atria. Such atrial tachycardias, or rapid heartbeats, can reduce blood pressure and cause fainting. But they're much less dangerous than those involving the ventricles, the heart's lower chambers, which pump blood to the body. Since the treatment depends on the cause, your mother-in-law needs to be evaluated with a 24-hour *Holter* monitor, which should provide a diagnosis if the problem recurs while she's wearing it.

## SURGERY FOR RACING HEART?

**Q** *Your article on atrial fibrillation didn't mention catheter ablation. Is that an effective treatment?*

**A** In many cases, yes. Atrial fibrillation is a rapid, irregular heartbeat caused by abnormal tissue in the heart muscle. The disorder can cause lightheadedness and fainting, and it increases the risk of heart failure and stroke. When medication fails to restore normal rhythms and there's no serious heart disease, a minimally invasive procedure called catheter ablation can be considered. During that procedure, a laser or radio-wave device is snaked through a vein up to the heart, where it destroys the abnormal tissue. That restores normal heartbeat in 70 to 90 percent of patients, though up to one-third may require additional procedures and up to one-fourth may still need drugs. About 1 to 2 percent of patients experience complications such as serious vein narrowing or blockage, transient ischemic attacks (tiny strokes), bleeding around the heart, or rhythm abnormalities requiring a pacemaker. Moreover, the long-term safety and effectiveness of catheter ablation are unknown.

## BLOCKED BUNDLE BRANCH

**Q** *I'm a 50-year-old male with a "right bundle branch block." Is that cause for concern?*

**A** Not necessarily. The bundle branches are fibers within the heart muscle that transmit nerve impulses, causing the right and left ventricles to contract and pump blood into the arteries. Occasionally, transmission in one of the bundles becomes blocked, probably due to a clot in a tiny blood vessel feeding the bundle. The affected ventricle then contracts later than the other ventricle; this shows up as a characteristic pattern on an electrocardiogram. There are usually no symptoms, and there's no treatment. A blocked bundle branch, particularly on the left, does increase the risk of subsequent heart attack somewhat. That risk is compounded by the presence of other risk factors for coronary heart disease: high blood-cholesterol levels, hypertension, male gender, diabetes, age, smoking, and a family history of coronary heart disease before age 50.

## ACCURATE ANGIOGRAM

**Q** Before I started a strenuous exercise program, my doctor ordered an exercise stress test to check my heart, even though I have no symptoms of coronary heart disease. That test was inconclusive, so I had a thallium stress test, which indicated some coronary disease. To confirm that finding, I underwent angiography, which found no sign of disease. Which test should I believe?

**A** Angiography. That procedure, in which the coronary arteries are injected with dye and examined by X-ray, is the most accurate test for blocked coronary arteries. The two stress tests are safer and less expensive than angiography, which is why they're generally done first. However, it is possible for those stress tests to turn up positive when there's actually nothing wrong.

---

## MITRAL VALVE PROLAPSE

**Q** I am in my mid-30s. A few years ago I was diagnosed as having a heart condition called mitral valve prolapse. What exactly is it, and does it make jogging or other exercise risky?

**A** Mitral valve prolapse (MVP) involves a ballooning of the heart's mitral valve leaflets or flaps, which control blood flow between the two left chambers of the heart. Recent improvements in taking and interpreting echocardiograms, or ultrasound images of the heart, have dramatically changed how doctors view MVP. They now know that MVP is far less common and risky than previously believed.

Individuals who've been told that they have MVP, particular more than two years ago, should ask their doctors to review the diagnosis. Those with true prolapse need to take special precautions—regular check-ups with a cardiologist and antibiotics before routine dental procedures—only if the echocardiogram shows that the mitral valve leaks (regurgitates) or that the flaps on the valve are unusually thick. As for exercise, most people with MVP can follow a sensible program. Ask your doctor for guidance.

## HEART PALPITATIONS

**Q** *I'm 62 and have had heart palpitations for years. What can you tell me about them?*

**A** "Palpitations" is a nonmedical term for any heart rhythm that feels abnormal. That can include extra beats, dropped beats, forceful beats, rapid beats, or irregular beats. For proper diagnosis the abnormality must first be "captured" on an electrocardiogram or on a 24-hour heartbeat recording. Palpitations can be caused by emotional stress, an overactive thyroid, certain medications, or diseases of the coronary arteries, heart muscle, or heart valves. Sometimes there's no detectable cause.

At some point soon you probably should have your palpitations checked, but first try eliminating a few things on your own—caffeine (coffee, tea, cocoa, chocolate, soda), nasal decongestants, appetite suppressants—and see if it makes a difference.

## ATYPICAL ANGINA?

**Q** *I've read that angina, the type of chest pain that signals coronary heart disease, is usually brought on by exercise and relieved by rest. I sometimes experience chest discomfort while resting but never while exercising. Could that discomfort still be angina?*

**A** It's unlikely. But an uncommon form of coronary disease can cause angina when you're resting or asleep—due to arterial spasm, not blockage. To rule out that possibility, your physician could have you wear a heart monitor for 24 hours. You should also have a treadmill exercise test, even though you haven't noticed the pain while exercising.

If those tests find no sign of coronary disease, your physician will investigate other possible causes of your discomfort. It's most likely to be a temporary problem, such as heartburn or spasms of the esophagus. Occasionally, however, the discomfort reflects a chronic disorder, such as a hiatal hernia or gallbladder disease.

## ✚ *Office* **Visit**

# COPING WITH RAPID, IRREGULAR HEARTBEAT

"ONE MINUTE I WAS FINE AND THEN, out of the blue, I felt this wild, irregular thrashing inside my chest, as if my heart was going to jump right out of my body. I became lightheaded and a little short of breath. I thought it was all over." That's how the 53-year-old advertising executive described his experience with atrial fibrillation, a common heart-rhythm disorder that affects about 2 million Americans.

Normal heartbeat is initiated when an electrical center in the wall of one of the heart's upper chambers (atria) sends an impulse to the lower chambers (ventricles), causing them to contract regularly in what is called normal sinus rhythm. If the initiating center begins firing in a hectic, chaotic manner, the result is atrial fibrillation, a rapid and irregular heartbeat, often as fast as 180 beats per minute.

Those fast, erratic beats don't let the heart chambers fill with or eject blood efficiently, so that less blood is pumped to the rest of the body. That can cause lightheadedness and sometimes fainting. Some fibrillation patients whose heart muscle has been compromised from a prior heart attack or longstanding high blood pressure can develop congestive heart failure.

But the most serious consequence is clot formation inside the atria. If those clots escape into the bloodstream, they can cause strokes or loss of circulation to a limb. Patients who fibrillate intermittently are at just as much risk for stroke as patients who fibrillate constantly.

## WHAT'S THE CAUSE?

Several conditions can cause atrial fibrillation: atrial enlargement (as a result of mitral-valve disease), an overactive thyroid, chronic lung disease, coronary disease, heart-muscle disease, and high blood pressure. Depending on their symptoms, patients with newly diagnosed atrial fibrillation may receive echocardiograms, thyroid tests, or nuclear stress tests to detect those conditions.

A few patients (like our ad executive), who have no apparent underlying cause, are called "lone fibrillators." Lone fibrillators under age 60 run less risk of stroke than their older counterparts or those with underlying diseases.

## TREATMENT CHOICES

Since stroke is its most devastating potential complication, everyone with atrial fibrillation (except, perhaps, lone fibrillators under age 60, who can be treated with aspirin) should probably take the blood thinner warfarin *(Coumadin)*. The only exceptions are patients with a recent bleeding ulcer, previous hemorrhagic stroke, or a blood-clotting defect.

For years, cardiologists have disagreed about what's more important—restoring normal, regular sinus rhythm or just slowing down the speeding heart rate, even if the rhythm remains somewhat erratic. The predominant view has been to spare no effort to convert the patient back to normal sinus rhythm and use drugs to try to maintain it. Conversion can be accomplished by electrically shocking the heart. In order to prevent recurrences, there's a formidable array of antiarrhythmic drugs, such as amiodarone, disopyramide, flecainide, and propafenone, which are expensive and can have significant side effects, some requiring hospitalization.

For a smaller group of cardiologists, the important thing is to control the heart rate, especially in patients whose symptoms are minimal or absent. Rate can be easily controlled with calcium-channel blockers (diltiazem, verapamil), beta-blockers (metoprolol, sotalol), or digoxin. (Those drugs can sometimes restore normal sinus rhythm as well.)

Some cardiologists straddle both camps, advocating at least one attempt at rhythm correction followed by rate control if fibrillation recurs. Recently two independent studies reported in The New England Journal of Medicine concluded that either approach is valid. Patients treated with rate control did just as well as patients treated with rhythm control. If anything, rate control—which is easier and cheaper—tended to produce better results.

## A HAPPY OUTCOME

Paramedics diagnosed the ad executive's atrial fibrillation in the ambulance and started him on aspirin and intravenous diltiazem. By the time he reached the hospital, he was in normal sinus rhythm. No abnormalities showed up on testing. Now, six months later, he continues on aspirin and oral diltiazem, and his heart rhythm remains normal.

---

## ✚ *Office* Visit

# CARDIAC REHAB: RUN FOR YOUR LIFE

"BOY, AM I GLAD THAT'S OVER!" My patient, a 58-year-old high-school math teacher, had just returned home after a triple-vessel coronary bypass. "I want to take it easy for a few months—maybe I'll head south and relax on a beach somewhere." He was taken aback when I told him that what he did over the next few months was crucial to his survival, and that it would involve hard work, not fun in the sun.

Cardiac rehabilitation would start immediately, even while his chest wound was still healing. I advised him to take short walks twice a day for the first three weeks. Our dietician coached him and his wife on the basics of a heart-healthy diet. About a month after his surgery, a nuclear stress test showed that his bypass grafts were functioning properly. I then referred him to a local cardiac rehab center, where he began the formal process of recovery—not from surgery but from the disease that had almost taken his life.

## NO REST FOR THE WEARY

Doctors used to tell patients recovering from an invasive heart procedure or a heart attack to rest in bed for a month or more. That often caused serious complications, such as inflamed leg veins, blood clots migrating to the lungs, and pneumonia. Those problems, plus the lack of evidence that prolonged bed rest did any good, led to progressively earlier mobilization and shorter hospital stays.

Today, heart-attack or coronary-bypass patients typically remain in the hospital for only about five days; patients who undergo angioplasty, or use of a tiny balloon to open a blocked coronary artery, are out in a day. Before discharge, virtually all heart-attack patients undergo stress testing to see whether any heart muscle remains in jeopardy. If so, a special X-ray of the arteries is taken to check whether angioplasty or bypass is needed.

## A MULTIPRONGED PROGRAM

Comprehensive cardiac rehabilitation begins as soon as the patient is stabilized, sometimes before the patient has left the hospital. Clinical trials have shown that such regimens reduce both the incidence of recurrent heart attack and the overall death rate by roughly 25 percent.

A comprehensive rehab program should include the following features:

• An ongoing relationship with a physician—preferably a cardiologist—well versed in caring for heart patients.

• Literature, videos, and classes to educate patients about the causes and prevention of coronary heart disease.

• A carefully supervised exercise program.

• A high-produce diet that's low in saturated fat, trans fat, and cholesterol.

• Permanent loss of excess weight.

• Reduction of blood pressure and blood cholesterol to optimal levels—such as less than 100 mg/dl of the "bad" LDL cholesterol—using drugs if necessary.

• Heart drugs to improve cardiac function and reduce the risk of heart attack.

• A low-dose aspirin regimen to help prevent artery-blocking blood clots.

## FINDING THE RIGHT FACILITY

The cornerstone of any cardiac rehab program is exercise, since it helps patients lose weight, lower their blood pressure, boost their "good" HDL cholesterol, and increase their capacity for physical activity. So choose an exercise facility carefully.

Although there doesn't appear to be any increased risk of heart attack or death during cardiac rehab, it's best for a physician or a nurse to be on hand in case problems arise. That's especially important during the first three months after angioplasty, bypass, or a heart attack, when minor abnormalities such as irregular heart rhythms often surface.

The facility should also have an exercise physiologist or at least knowledgeable exercise assistants available. Those professionals monitor electrocardiograms, blood pressures, pulse rates, and symptoms before and after exercise, to chart your progress and detect any adverse events. They report that information to your physician, who can alter your program or change your drug regimen as needed.

In addition, look for an exercise facility that offers an assortment of aerobic-exercise machines. The atmosphere should be relaxed; the personnel, friendly and helpful.

After the initial 12 weeks, most rehab patients graduate from the supervised program to a less formal regimen that should take an hour or so of their time at least three times a week, either at home or in a facility.

When I saw our math teacher just a few weeks ago, he was into the eighth month of his lifelong rehab program. He told me that he was enthusiastically encouraging all his friends to follow a heart-healthy lifestyle. He hoped he wasn't offending any bypass surgeons.

## Children's health

### STRENGTH TRAINING: SAFE FOR KIDS

**Q** *I've always heard that muscle-building exercise will "stunt a child's growth." Now I hear it's recommended for children. Is strength training safe for kids?*

**A** It won't inhibit growth under any circumstances, but it can cause injury—usually when lifting heavy weights with incorrect form. However, if it's carefully supervised and correctly done, strength training can actually reduce the risk of sports injuries in youngsters, since greater muscular strength and endurance help protect the joints and tendons. With proper safeguards, strength training can start whenever a child shows interest in the activity.

### TONSIL TROUBLE

**Q** *My 9-year-old daughter has had swollen tonsils almost every month for the past two years. Our pediatrician repeatedly prescribes an antibiotic, which does help. I know tonsils no longer are removed routinely, but I wonder whether something more than a prescription is in order. Should I be so concerned?*

**A** Tonsillitis is usually caused by a strep infection and (when it's strep) is treated with antibiotics. Your daughter is a demonstration of how far the pendulum of medical opinion has swung away from the other treatment, tonsillectomy. Years ago there would have been no question. She would have been among the million people each year, most of them children, who had their tonsils removed. Today the number of operations is only about one-fourth as great; hers is a borderline case.

Surgery is certainly not necessary for your child as long as her tonsils are not so swollen that they obstruct breathing or swallowing. Instead, the American Academy of Pediatrics says surgery is "a reasonable option" for a child who has many severe sore throats, especially if they are caused by strep.

How much will it help? For children with frequent sore throats, the operation has been shown to reduce the number of sore throats for a couple of years; after that the improvement appears to be slight. Considering the costs and risks, surgery might be indicated if she's now missing a significant amount of school.

## WHICH MILK FOR KIDS?

**Q** *What's the best milk for our 4-year-old? My wife says whole, the doctor says 2 percent, and I say 1 percent or skim milk. I contend that the difference in calories can be made up by offering more nutritious snacks.*

**A** The only firm rules are for infants: The American Academy of Pediatrics recommends no cow's milk under age 1 and no reduced-fat milk under age 2. After children turn 2 and their need for fat diminishes, many pediatricians recommend switching to 1 percent (low fat) or 2 percent milk (reduced fat). That's a good compromise between a child's need for a reliable, nutritious source of calories and the desire to instill a low-fat diet as a lifelong habit. However, doctors may modify their advice when a child is obese, is failing to thrive, or has an elevated risk of cardiovascular disease.

## CONSTIPATED CHILD

**Q** *For the past six months our 3-year-old son has averaged five days or more between bowel movements. We've tried to give him lots of natural fiber and fluids. On the advice of our pediatrician, we gave our son a stool softener for three weeks, but it hasn't helped. Should we keep using it?*

**A** Prolonged use of a stool softener in children is not a good idea. Constipation in a 3-year-old is a common problem. In addition to lack of fiber or fluid in the diet, possible causes include resistance to toilet training, painful anal fissures, or even Hirschsprung's disease (a lack of muscle tone in part of the colon). Ask your pediatrician to refer you to a pediatric gastroenterologist, who may be better able to diagnose and treat the problem.

---

## BED-WETTING

**Q** *My 11-year-old daughter occasionally wets her bed. Why is this happening, and what can we do about it?*

**A** In most cases, the cause of bed wetting is unknown. However, psychological stress from such changes as the birth of a sibling or separation from a parent is often responsible. That's especially likely if the child has begun to wet the bed again a year or more after being successfully toilet trained. Rarely is bed-wetting caused by an underlying disorder, such as diabetes, infection, or seizures.

Once a physical problem has been ruled out, handle bed-wetting with gentle measures. Avoid mechanical devices that use frightening alarms or electric shocks. Limit fluids after supper. Be sure your daughter urinates just before bedtime. Wake her up to urinate several hours after she's gone to sleep. Praise and reward her for a dry night; don't scold or punish for a wet night. If the problem persists, a brief course of the drug imipramine *(Tofranil)* can help a child gain control by helping to close the urethral sphincter, the muscle that stops the flow of urine. The use of an inhaled diuretic hormone desmopressin *(DDAVP, Stimate)* at bedtime has recently become the treatment of choice. Even if all those measures fail, most children outgrow bed-wetting by adolescence.

## Cholesterol

### GREAT CHOLESTEROL, CLOGGED ARTERIES

**Q** *My mother, who's in her 70s, has a great lipid profile: a low total-cholesterol level, a high level of the "good" HDL cholesterol, and low triglycerides. And she exercises every day. (On the down side, she is a bit nervous and has high blood pressure, which medication keeps under control.) Yet tests recently revealed partial blockage of a coronary artery. What else can she do to keep her heart healthy?*

**A** Partially blocked coronary arteries are common for a woman of your mother's age. While blockage occurs most often in people with such risk factors as smoking, diabetes, obesity, physical inactivity, and unfavorable lipid levels, it can also occur in people without these conditions. There are some potentially helpful steps your mother could take.

Most important, all coronary patients should ask their doctor about taking daily low-dose aspirin to help prevent blood clots, which can trigger a heart attack. In addition, eating plenty of fruits, vegetables, and whole grains will supply lots of possibly heart-shielding antioxidants as well as B vitamins, which help control levels of a potentially heart-harming protein called homocysteine. (Such a diet may help fend off cancer as well.) Your mother should also consider taking a daily supplement containing 3 to 6 micrograms of vitamin B12 (which many people over age 50 cannot absorb adequately from food). And she may want to consider various relaxation techniques to reduce excessive stress, a likely coronary risk factor. Finally, if her "bad" LDL cholesterol is higher than 100 milligrams per deciliter—"great" for the normal population, but still too high for a coronary patient—she needs to lower her LDL further.

## FEED YOUR "GOOD" CHOLESTEROL?

**Q** *What foods should I eat to raise my "good" HDL but not my "bad" LDL cholesterol?*

**A** Individual foods can't do much for your HDL, which fights heart disease by dragging cholesterol out of the arteries. Only a few dietary items, notably alcoholic beverages and possibly grape juice, may increase HDL, and then only slightly. In contrast, regular aerobic exercise can boost HDL substantially.

But reducing your LDL, which dumps cholesterol into arteries, protects your heart more effectively—and there are several good ways to do that. Proven dietary steps include eating less saturated fat (mainly from animal foods), trans fat (from partially hydrogenated oils), cholesterol (from eggs and meat) and more soluble fiber (from produce, legumes, and oats). Consuming soy foods and possibly plant sterols (from margarines such as *Benecol* or *Take Control)* may help, too. Nondietary steps include losing weight and building muscle.

## ARE TRIGLYCERIDES A THREAT?

**Q** *What are triglycerides, and can they really harm my health?*

**A** They're an abundant type of fat in the bloodstream. Excess amounts can increase the risk of heart attack and stroke directly, by helping to clog the arteries and promoting blood clots. They can also increase risk indirectly, in two ways. The liver converts excess triglycerides into the "bad," artery-clogging LDL cholesterol. And triglycerides tend to displace the "good," artery-clearing HDL cholesterol from the proteins that haul fats through the blood.

So people should try to keep their triglyceride level below 150 milligrams per deciliter (mg/dl). Steps that can lower triglycerides include losing excess weight; cutting back on saturated fat, sugar, other carbohydrates, and dietary cholesterol; minimizing alcohol intake; exercising regularly; stopping smoking; and keeping diabetes well controlled. Prescription drugs such as fenofibrate *(Tricor)* and gemfibrozil *(Lopid)* are sometimes necessary to lower extremely high triglyceride levels (over 400 mg/dl), which can harm the pancreas.

## LOWER DOSAGE, FEWER SIDE EFFECTS?

**Q** *After taking 20 milligrams of pravastatin* (Pravachol) *daily for a year, I have now brought my cholesterol level under control. I want to lower my dosage to 10 mg to minimize possible side effects, but my doctor says the higher dosage poses no additional risk. Is that true?*

**A** Yes. In theory the lower the dosage of any medication, the lower the risk of side effects and the lower the cost. But with the change you're considering, any decrease in that risk would be minimal, particularly if you're not experiencing any side effects at your current dosage. And any possible benefit might be outweighed by a reduction in the medication's cholesterol-lowering effect. As for cost, the smaller dose would save you only about 15 cents per day.

## CONFUSION OVER HDL AND LDL

*You seem to discuss HDL and LDL as if they were two types of cholesterol. But then you say that both HDL and LDL transport cholesterol. I'm confused.*

The terminology is confusing. HDL (high-density lipoprotein) and LDL (low-density lipoprotein) are not types of cholesterol. Rather, they're fat-protein compounds that transport cholesterol through the blood. (HDL tends to carry cholesterol away from the arteries, thus earning the title of "good" cholesterol; LDL, or "bad" cholesterol, tends to deposit cholesterol in the walls of arteries.) Sometimes, though, HDL and LDL are used as shorthand terms to refer to the lipoproteins together with their cholesterol cargo.

## CHOLESTEROL LEVELS IN OLDER PEOPLE

*I'm 84 years old, and my total cholesterol level is 245. To my amazement, a doctor recently stated that the higher one's cholesterol, the longer one lives. Do the latest studies support this?*

No. Cholesterol levels alone, of course, do not determine one's life expectancy. However, a few surprising studies in the early 1990s did find a reduced association between elevated serum-cholesterol levels and coronary heart disease in older people. On the basis of those epidemiologic studies, some researchers have specu-

lated that it may not be worthwhile to measure and reduce cholesterol levels in people older than 75. But recently scientists from the
National Heart, Lung, and Blood Institute reviewed the evidence
and issued new federal guidelines. "If a patient older than 75 years
with coronary heart disease is otherwise in relatively good health,
cholesterol-lowering therapy can be given serious consideration," it
said. The bottom line is that it's never too late to start managing high
serum-cholesterol levels in older patients.

## NIACIN ALERT

*I recently read that the sustained-release form of niacin,
which I've been taking to control my blood cholesterol, can
cause liver damage. Why is this form of niacin dangerous, but the
regular crystalline form, which causes me to flush, is not?*

It's long been known that both crystalline (short-
acting) and sustained-release niacin can damage the liver at
high doses. It now seems that the sustained-release form can cause
liver injury even at low therapeutic doses. In several case reports,
people who had recovered from such damage were then given
crystalline niacin with no ill effects. The reason for the difference
is unclear; it may be that taking short-acting crystalline niacin allows the liver to recover between doses while slow-release niacin
affects liver enzyme systems for longer durations and with fewer
recovery periods. Another report suggests that high doses of niacin
can aggravate diabetes and may induce the disease in borderline
diabetics. Although niacin is available without a prescription, it
should nevertheless be taken under a doctor's supervision and only
in crystalline form. Increasing the dosage very slowly to the target
level will minimize any uncomfortable facial flushing.

## DRUGS AND GRAPEFRUIT

**Q** *I take atorvastatin (Lipitor) for high cholesterol and nifedipine (Procardia XL) for angina every day. Is there any danger in eating grapefruit while taking those?*

**A** There could be. Several compounds in grapefruit can inactivate an intestinal enzyme that controls the absorption of statin drugs, such as atorvastatin, and calcium-channel blockers, such as nifedipine. That can cause potentially harmful increases of those drugs in the blood levels. So don't start consuming grapefruit or grapefruit juice while taking them. But if you've already been doing so, with good results and no signs of overdose, it may be wise to stick with the combination; abandoning the grapefruit could lead to reduced absorption and inadequate blood levels of the drug. Note that grapefruit can similarly interact with the anticonvulsant carbamazepine *(Tegretol)* and the antidepressant clomipramine *(Anafranil)*.

## EATING BEFORE CHOLESTEROL TESTS

**Q** *I had my cholesterol tested recently at a health fair. The previous day, I ate two meals with lots of fat and cholesterol. Did that throw off my cholesterol reading?*

**A** No. Levels of total cholesterol don't change much from day to day. So you don't have to fast or worry about what you eat the day before a test. But if you were having blood drawn for a complete lipid analysis, including HDL cholesterol and triglycerides, then a 12- to 14-hour fast would be required.

## JUMPING CHOLESTEROL

**Q** *According to a finger-prick test, my blood-cholesterol level was 197. Two months later, it was 272 on a fasting blood workup. My diet didn't change during that time. Is such a jump possible in only two months?*

**A** No. Cholesterol readings cannot vary that much, that soon. The finger-prick test was probably wrong. Squeezing the fingertip to draw blood produces secretions that dilute the blood and can lead to a falsely low reading.

## CHOLESTEROL AND COFFEE . . .

**Q** *I've read that unfiltered brewed coffee can raise blood-cholesterol levels. But what about instant coffee?*

**A** Apparently not. That's because the manufacturing process removes nearly all of the two compounds—cafestol and kahweol—responsible for the increased cholesterol levels.

## . . . AND DECAF

**Q** *Does decaffeinated coffee contain the compounds that can raise cholesterol levels?*

**A** That depends solely on how it's prepared. The decaffeination process itself has no effect on the offending substances—cafestol and kahweol. But like regular coffee, decaf that's instant or drip-filtered will have virtually none of those chemicals.

# Colon and rectal complaints

## HEMORRHOID RELIEF

**Q** *I've suffered from hemorrhoids for years, and recently some of them may have prolapsed. Can drugs cure them, or should I consider surgery?*

**A** Unfortunately, no drugs can cure hemorrhoids, those sometimes painful clumps of blood vessels that erupt from the lining of the rectum. The problem worsens when the clumps prolapse, or protrude outside the anus. But you probably won't need surgery, which requires hospitalization and costs several thousand dollars. That's typically reserved for problems such as pain, incontinence, bleeding, or ulceration.

First, try the following simple and usually effective remedies: Consuming more fiber and water, and taking a stool-softening drug such as docusate *(Colace, Surfak)* can help prevent worsening. To ease the irritation, sit in a warm bath, use a general-purpose wet wipe, and apply a water-based (nonpetroleum) ointment such as K-Y Jelly. (Those products are just as effective as the special hemorrhoid ointments and wipes sold in drugstores.) For temporary relief, take acetaminophen *(Tylenol)*—not aspirin or ibuprofen *(Advil)*, which can promote bleeding. And try to gently push the prolapsed hemorrhoids back into the rectum after each bowel movement.

If those steps fail, discuss nonsurgical removal with your doctor; it's an office procedure costing a few hundred dollars. The most effective procedure uses special rubber bands that cut off blood flow to the hemorrhoids, which fall off in a week or so. Other techniques destroy the clumps with infrared or radio waves.

## DIVERTICULOSIS DIET

**Q** *I'm a 73-year-old man with diverticulosis, and I've been told to avoid nuts, the skins of raw vegetables, fruits, corn, and peas. All of these have lots of roughage and are very nutritious. I wonder whether avoiding them makes sense.*

**A** You're right to wonder; the advice you've received is out of date. It used to be thought that roughage aggravated diverticulosis—small pouches in the colon that develop in more than a third of people over age 60. It's now clear that the opposite is true. People with your condition are encouraged to eat a diet high in fiber, ideally more than 30 grams a day. As you already realize, the foods you've been told to avoid are excellent sources.

## DIET AND DIVERTICULOSIS

**Q** *Like many people my age (over 50), I have diverticulosis. My doctor has told me not to eat seeds and nuts and to avoid constipation. But I know people with the same problem who have been told to eat, avoid, or do different things. Could you provide some insight into this problem?*

**A** Diverticulosis is a common condition in which the inner lining of the intestine protrudes into the intestinal wall, forming small pouches in the wall of the colon. It affects one in four people by the age of 50 and is nearly universal by the age of 80. It's believed that our modern low-fiber diet is at least partly to blame.

Diverticulosis usually doesn't cause any symptoms, but some people with the condition do experience bloating, cramps, and changed bowel habits, such as constipation, diarrhea, or alternating attacks of both. Abdominal pain (especially low on the left side) accompanied by fever might signal the development of diverticulitis, an infection of the pouches. That can lead to abscess formation and to perforation of the bowel, which can cause peritonitis, a generalized infection of the abdominal lining.

To avoid those problems, switch gradually to a higher-fiber diet with more whole grains, fruits, and vegetables.

## ANAL ITCHING

**Q** *I have been suffering from severe pruritus ani for nearly a year. To find relief from the itching, I've been to a family physician, a proctologist, four dermatologists, and an allergist. So far, no treatment has helped. Do you know of anything that might relieve my discomfort?*

**A** Since you've already seen seven doctors, they've probably ruled out the most common causes of anal itching: worms, hemorrhoids, fungal infections, skin fissures, sweating, irritants in food, and poor anal hygiene.

One possibility that's sometimes overlooked is neurodematitis. This is not an actual nerve disorder but rather a lengthy cycle of itching and repeated scratching. It leads to gradual thickening of the skin around the anus, which then itches more than ever.

If neurodermatitis is indeed the cause of your condition, it may gradually abate if you force yourself not to scratch the thickened skin. When you're at home, applying an ice-cold compress to the irritated area can ease the urge to scratch. Since many sufferers scratch when they're asleep, you should keep your fingernails short and even wear soft mittens to bed. A hypnotist or psychotherapist might help you stop scratching.

## BLOOD IN THE STOOL

*Q* *Microscopic traces of blood have been detected in my stool. Sigmoidoscopy revealed internal hemorrhoids near the entrance of the anus. Does this mean surgery, even though I've had no discomfort?*

*A* Not necessarily. Stool softeners *(Colace, Surfak)* or psyllium laxatives *(Metamucil, Mylanta Natural Fiber)* can reduce straining during bowel movements and may help stop the bleeding, just as they help prevent anal fissures. Antihemorrhoidal creams and suppositories are not particularly helpful for this problem. Like persistent fissures, persistent bleeding may require surgery. A colonoscopy should be done to rule out bleeding sources beyond the reach of a sigmoidoscope.

## COLONOSCOPY PAIN

*Q* *Because of a strong family history of colon cancer, doctors have advised me to have an annual colonoscopy. I've undergone the procedure a few times and found the pain nearly unbearable. My gastroenterologist says he doesn't give painkillers for colonoscopy. Is there anything that would help me cope with this ordeal?*

*A* Yes—drugs, including those painkillers. Without them, the colonoscope causes discomfort and sometimes pain as it snakes through and stretches your colon. Before the procedure, most gastroenterologists give intravenous narcotics to kill pain and tranquilizers to relax you and your colon. If you can't persuade your gastroenterologist to administer such medications, try another gastroenterologist.

## ULCERATIVE COLITIS

**Q** *I recently found out I have ulcerative colitis. What's the latest on the cause and treatment of this disease?*

**A** Physicians still don't know what causes ulcerative colitis, an inflammatory disease of the colon that leads to diarrhea and rectal bleeding. (It can also affect the skin, eyes, joints, and liver.) However, various drugs can suppress the inflammation and control the symptoms. Those medications include mesalamine *(Asacol)* and sulfasalazine *(Azulfidine)*, corticosteroid drugs such as prednisone *(Deltasone)*, and in resistant cases, immunosuppressant drugs such as mercaptopurine *(Purinethol)*.

People who have had extensive ulcerative colitis for a long time are at increased risk of colon cancer. Those people should undergo annual colonoscopy (inspection of the entire colon through a flexible lighted tube) to check for cancer or precancerous changes.

## Cysts, lumps, and tumors

## BENIGN BUMP OR PERILOUS GROWTH?

**Q** *I have a small, hard, brown bump on my leg. My doctor says it should probably be removed. But my dermatologist says it's a harmless dermatofibroma. Should I be worried?*

**A** Not if it's really a dermatofibroma. Those knots of benign fibrous tissue commonly appear on the legs where the skin has been mildly inflamed, by an insect bite or splinter, for example. Though often confused with moles, those nodules are harder, may itch, and are sometimes purple or red. And unlike potentially cancerous skin growths, they don't change shape or color, are uniformly colored, have clearly defined edges, and generally don't bleed. Removal is not only unnecessary but can also leave a scar larger than the original bump.

## BODY BUMPS

**Q** *I have several egg-shaped growths on my body. Please explain whether these bumps, diagnosed as lipomas, are dangerous and how the condition can be treated. I would have quite a few scars if the lumps were all surgically removed.*

**A** Lipomas are benign, fatty tumors that are fairly common, typically appearing on the trunk, neck, and forearms. Usually they cause no discomfort and are best left alone. If you prefer to have them removed for cosmetic reasons, you can choose either conventional surgery or liposuction, in which a small tube inserted under the skin sucks out the fatty tissue, resulting in less scar formation. The rare lipoma that enlarges rapidly may harbor a cancerous growth, known as a liposarcoma, and should be removed surgically.

## BENIGN CHANGES IN THE BREAST

**Q** *Six months ago I had a breast biopsy that showed benign changes—fibrocystic disease and intraductal hyperplasia. Is either of these linked to an increased risk of breast cancer in the absence of a family history?*

**A** Your risk of breast cancer is no greater than average. The conditions you mention are natural changes that occur over time.

Fibrocystic "disease," a term that implies an abnormality or disorder, is a misnomer, since about half of all premenopausal women have it. It's really a catchall term for painful, lumpy breasts. Such lumps were once thought to be associated with increased cancer risk, but several studies have since dispelled that notion. Intraductal hyperplasia is a benign overgrowth of cells in the breast ducts, the tubes that carry milk to the nipple. Only when those cells start to appear abnormal on a biopsy does the risk of cancer increase.

## Dental care

### FLUORIDE SUPPLEMENTS

**Q** *Are sodium fluoride supplements safe for my 2-year-old child?*

**A** Yes, in the correct dosage. Fluoride supplements (drops or tablets) may be prescribed for children when the fluoride content of local drinking water is less than 0.3 parts per million. The recommended daily dosage is 0.25 milligram from six months to the age of three, 0.5 milligram from age three to six, and 1 milligram from age six to age 16, when the second molars have usually erupted fully. After that, fluoride from toothpaste and fluoride treatments at the dentist's office provide sufficient protection. Some years ago, when the recommended dosage for children up to age two was higher (0.5 milligram), there was some concern about mild dental fluorosis—faint white spots on the teeth. But that minor side effect rarely occurs today.

## GENTLE GUM CARE

**Q** *My dentist recently recommended that I use a* Water Pik *oral irrigator. SInce I've used it at near-maximum pressure, my gums have stopped bleeding. But your recent report on tooth care stressed the importance of gentle cleaning. Does that apply to my new device as well?*

**A** Yes. Intense water pressure can force bacteria through the thin walls of the gums, especially if you have a periodontal pocket, or space between the gums and teeth. (Pockets are often present if the gums have been bleeding a lot.) Such spread of bacteria can lead to a more serious condition, such as severe inflammation or even an infection that spreads beyond the gums. So if you're using an oral irrigator regularly, don't set it at more than half power—which should still be enough to improve your oral health. And remember, water treatment doesn't take the place of daily brushing and flossing, which are still the most effective self-care steps for keeping your gums and teeth clean enough to help ward off gum disease and tooth decay.

## CALCIUM FOR ORAL HEALTH?

**Q** *I'm a 42-year-old woman with receding gums and bone loss around my teeth. My dentist recommends that I take calcium supplements to delay further bone loss. Is this the best treatment for my condition?*

**A** There's no evidence that getting extra calcium will help reduce periodontal disease, which is what causes such bone loss. You should be evaluated by a periodontist. Treatment options range from periodic root planing to various surgical therapies.

## ANTIBIOTICS BEFORE DENTAL WORK

**Q** *Ever since I had a total hip replacement, my surgeon has recommended antibiotics before I have dental work. My dentist says that's no longer necessary. Who's right?*

**A** That depends. Joint-replacement patients may need antibiotics before dental procedures likely to cause bleeding, such as tooth extraction, root canal, and even routine cleaning. That's because bacteria in the mouth can enter the bloodstream via the wounds and possibly infect a recently implanted joint. Most people need that precaution only during the first two years following the operation. After that, it's generally required only if you have weakened immunity or a history of infection in the new joint.

## DENTAL X-RAYS

**Q** *I'm 40 years old and haven't had a cavity since I was 10. Yet my dentist recommends annual X-rays to look between back teeth for cavities. Doesn't this expose me to too much radiation?*

**A** Overall, the risk from dental X-rays is minimal. Today, a full mouth series of X-rays exposes patients to only 13 millirems of radiation. By comparison, Americans are exposed to 300 millirems a year just from the natural environment. But if you have no history of cavities and your gums are healthy, there's little reason for annual X-rays. Talk to your dentist about having "bite–wing" X-rays every two or three years; they target the specific teeth the dentist is concerned about.

## SPECIAL TOOTHPASTE FOR TENDER TEETH?

**Q** *Some of my teeth hurt when I brush, even though I have no cavities or gum disease. I'm considering one of those special toothpastes for sensitive teeth. Do they really work?*

**A** Yes. Such pain usually stems from gum recession, which exposes the sensitive roots. The special pastes contain chemicals that can block that pain. Since brushing too hard can increase gum loss and sensitivity, use a soft-bristle brush and a gentle touch. And avoid whitening or stain-removing toothpastes, which can be more abrasive. If those steps don't help after a few weeks, your dentist may treat the problem teeth with a fluoride gel, a varnish, or a bonding agent.

## ✚ *Office* **Visit**

# BRISTLING IN THE TOOTHBRUSH AISLE

WITH IRWIN D. MANDEL, D.D.S.

EVEN AS A DENTIST, I find myself intimidated by the mob of new toothbrushes that crowd the shelves, featuring oversized handles with bumps, twists, and curves as well as bristles with differing angles, heights, and arrangements. Then there's the proliferating array of electric toothbrushes with confusingly different features. Unfortunately, researchers have not reliably determined whether any of the new brushes or features clean teeth better than the rest. But that doesn't mean you're at the mercy of the advertisers' conflicting claims. Certain traditional guidelines can still help you decide which brush to choose. Other research can help you determine when you'd benefit from buying an electric. Still other findings may spur you to improve your brushing enough to make the choice of toothbrush largely irrelevant.

## CHANGE THE BRUSHER, NOT THE BRUSH

It doesn't matter much which toothbrush you buy if you use it properly. In one carefully designed study, a dental professional cleaned each of 24 volunteers' teeth with eight of the newer manual toothbrushes. None of the brushes removed significantly more plaque—the sticky bacteria-laden deposits that cause tooth decay and gum disease—better than the others did. In fact, a 1998 CONSUMER REPORTS study found that a manual brush cleaned better than 13 electric models when users applied the right technique. (When they don't brush right, the opposite is true: Electrics typically outperform manuals.)

For best manual results, keep the bristles angled 45 degrees toward the gumline. If the brush head won't fit horizontally to clean the inside surfaces of the front teeth, turn it vertically. Holding the bristle tips in one spot against the gums and teeth, vibrate the brush head with a short back-and-forth or rotary motion. Then move on to the adjacent teeth. To avoid damaging the gums or any exposed root surfaces, brush no more than twice a day for two to three minutes, holding the toothbrush gently. (And floss at least once a day, to clean where your brush can't.)

For electrics, the right method varies from model to model. But even electric brushing should be done for a full two minutes and be paired with flossing.

Most people brush incorrectly and perfunctorily—significantly less than the optimal two to three minutes per session. So it's important to ask your dentist or hygienist to demonstrate the correct brushing (and flossing) method and to periodically check your technique. But some people are unable or unwilling to apply the right technique. For them, studies have shown that the current powered devices clean significantly better than manual brushes. Unlike earlier electrics, which might possibly harm the gums, the newer ones exert less force than manuals typically do. The newer manual products are designed to compensate for poor brushing, and studies sponsored by manufacturers suggest that one model or another may offer an advantage under those circumstances. So if your oral hygiene remains subpar after you've tried improving your technique, you may want to try an electric or possibly one of the newer manuals.

## SHOPPING TIPS

Whether you're seeking a manual or an electric, you'll have to experiment and get feedback from your dentist or hygienist: None of the studies of individual products has included a sufficiently broad range of brushes to draw reliable conclusions about which ones work best. Without such definitive evidence, the general recommendations of a major dental conference held some years ago still stand:

• Choose a brush whose size and shape let you comfortably reach every tooth.

• Avoid brush heads or handles so large that they substantially stretch your mouth, particularly if you're susceptible to canker sores.

• Choose soft nylon bristles (not medium or hard) with rounded tips, especially if the root surfaces are exposed. If they're sensitive, try ultrasoft bristles.

• Consider a large-handled brush with a special grip if you want a firmer hold—provided you don't start brushing harder, which can erode the gums.

Two more-recent tips on electrics:

• A built-in timer is a useful feature, which can help you avoid the widespread tendency to brush too briefly.

• Battery-powered brushes are appealing because of their low price, though they haven't been adequately tested against the costlier plug-in models.

## ✚ *Office* **Visit**

# WHEN TO GET A SECOND OPINION

WITH IRWIN D. MANDEL, D.D.S.

EXCEPT FOR A SHOT OF LIDOCAINE, nothing makes patients feel numb faster than being told they need major dental work. That initial shock is certainly understandable. After all, when your dentist recommends caps, tooth extractions, implants, or other extensive and irreversible changes to your mouth, you're faced with a significant—and usually very expensive—health decision.

Your dentist should take the time to explain the pros and cons of the procedure and should also inform you about other treatment options. But before you accept that recommendation, I'd advise you to consider seeking a second opinion. At the very least you'll feel reassured about undergoing the procedure if another dentist—particularly one who specializes in your specific problem—confirms that initial recommendation. A specialist may also tell you about options your own dentist didn't consider.

Many patients are reluctant to seek a second opinion for fear they'll offend their dentist. Granted, some dentists may bristle, but most would acknowledge that you'll be a better-informed patient for having gained that added perspective—and thus better prepared to make the right treatment choice.

## RED FLAGS

A second opinion is warranted any time you have doubts about a recommended procedure. Always consult a specialist whenever you're given a recommendation for major dental work that doesn't involve trying more conservative approaches first or that falls outside the norms of standard dentistry. Some specific recommendations that should prompt you to seek a second opinion include:

• Pulling an infected or painful tooth rather than opting for root canal, which almost always can save the tooth.

• Removing an impacted wisdom tooth that's not causing discomfort or other problems. One thorough analysis published in 1996 found that only 12 percent of wisdom teeth (teeth so firmly lodged in the jawbone that they can't break through the surface of the gum) ever cause problems after age 30. If X-rays reveal no underlying problem, leave the tooth alone.

• Using surgery to treat periodontal disease without first attempting a less invasive and often highly effective approach such as root planing and scaling (a deeper, more-thorough cleaning of periodontal pockets), possibly in combination with local antibacterial therapy.

• Treating jaw-joint pain (temporomandibular disorder) with braces, crowns, extensive grinding, jaw surgery, or other permanent changes rather than with conservative, reversible treatments, such as a plastic bite plate worn at night.

• Removing amalgam fillings because of worries over mercury toxicity. Despite misleading news reports to the contrary, research to date refutes that concern.

• Controversial, questionable, or disproved treatments for pain—such as aromatherapy, cranial manipulation, or reflexology. There's no evidence that those treatments provide any benefit.

## NARROWING THE CHOICES

Given the many techniques and materials now available, patients often find themselves having to choose among an array of treatment options. A specialist's guidance can be invaluable in helping you resolve difficult choices such as these:

• A fixed bridge vs. a removable partial denture to replace several missing teeth.

• Dentures that fit onto implants vs. dentures that fit directly onto the gums.

- New fillings vs. caps to replace old, worn-out fillings.
- Bonding vs. orthodontics to improve the appearance of teeth.

Don't be surprised if the specialist's opinion agrees with your dentist's; that's often the case. If they differ, or if you're still unsure, ask both to explain the reasons behind their recommendations, and weigh those reasons carefully.

## WHERE TO TURN FOR ADDED INPUT

Your dentist can point you toward a qualified specialist. But for a truly independent opinion, ask a physician, nurse, social worker, or other health professional you know for the name of a respected specialist. Or ask a nearby dental school or the dental department of a local hospital to put you in touch with its consultative service for your specific concern, or with a specialist on staff. When contacting the specialist, make it clear that you're seeking a second opinion.

## Diabetes

### ASPIRIN AND DIABETICS

**Q**  *Is it true that aspirin can lower blood-sugar levels in diabetics?*

**A**  Yes, but only with prolonged use and in large amounts (eight or more 325-milligram tablets a day). That reduction in blood-sugar levels can magnify the sugar-lowering effects of insulin and oral antidiabetic drugs. While such use of aspirin is generally safe for people with diabetes, they must be monitored closely by a physician.

## DIABETES DRUGS RISKY?

**Q** *My doctor insists that I take* DiaBeta *twice a day. But I have read that oral antidiabetic medications boost the risk of heart disease. What should I do?*

**A** Take the medication. That old warning was based on a single, seriously flawed study conducted many years ago. Untreated, diabetes results in persistently elevated blood-sugar levels, which can damage the eyes, heart, kidneys, and nerves. Those complications pose a much graver danger than any possible harm from the medication itself.

---

**✚ *Office* Visit**

# THE OTHER DIABETES

A 43-YEAR-OLD KINDERGARTEN TEACHER was referred to me after three miserable months of frequent urination and a thirst so incessant that she constantly carried a bottle of water. This plus her recent weight loss would have made her a classic case of Type I diabetes mellitus, except for one catch: Her blood sugars were normal and there was no sugar in her urine, negating that diagnosis.

Instead, she turned out to have an uncommon—and easier to manage—disorder known as diabetes insipidus.

### WHAT'S IN A NAME?
Whereas the most common diabetes mellitus stems from an abnormality in the pancreas, kidney malfunction is the immediate culprit in diabetes insipidus. When operating normally, our two

kidneys filter four ounces of blood every minute, remove the toxins and return about 99 percent of the cleansed fluid back to the body. What's left is excreted as urine. This important process is called concentrating the urine. When it fails, the body pours out large quantities of dilute urine and rapidly dehydrates if you don't drink copious amounts of fluid.

Diabetes mellitus also results in frequent urination, caused by the high glucose content of the urine. In the days before lab tests, doctors had to taste the urine to tell the difference between the two disorders. The sugar-laden urine of diabetes mellitus is sweet ("mellitus" being a Latin term for sweetened), whereas the dilute urine of the other diabetes is tasteless, or insipid.

## WHAT'S AT FAULT?

The ability of kidneys to concentrate urine depends on a substance aptly called antidiuretic hormone (ADH). Made in the brain and stored in the pituitary gland, ADH is sensitive to hydration changes. If we drink too much its release is inhibited so that we can easily excrete the added fluid and not get overhydrated. When we don't drink enough fluids, ADH is released and prompts the kidneys to reabsorb more water so we don't get dehydrated. Any glitch in this system will cause the kidneys to lose their urine-concentrating ability.

One rare cause is an inherited condition called nephrogenic diabetes insipidus, which may not become apparent until adulthood. Drugs that can impair the kidneys' ability to respond to ADH include lithium (most commonly used to treat manic-depressive illness), amphotericin B (for severe fungal infections), demeclocycline (an antibiotic), and methoxyflurane (an anesthetic gas). Any disorder or medication that causes a prolonged hike in blood calcium levels or low potassium blood levels can also paralyze the kidneys' ability to reabsorb water.

But the problem is usually at the other end of the system: a defect in the brain's ability to produce proper quantities of ADH.

## REACHING A DIAGNOSIS

The method used in the diagnosis of diabetes insipidus, the water deprivation test, has not changed for decades. It's uncomfortable, but doesn't take long and usually provides the answer. I hospitalized our schoolteacher for the day and, as the test's name suggested, prohibited her from drinking so much as a drop of water. I even disconnected the faucets in her room's sink so she wouldn't be tempted to cheat. We took hourly urine specimens that were tested for concentration and weighed her to measure urine loss. In five hours she lost nearly five pounds of fluid and also failed to concentrate her urine, thus securing the diagnosis. I then gave her an injection of synthetic ADH to see whether her kidneys responded normally. They did, which ruled out nephrogenic diabetes insipidus as the cause of her symptoms.

On direct questioning her husband eventually recalled that she had struck her head on the car door about two weeks prior to the onset of her symptoms, a mishap that she thought nothing of at the time. An MRI of her brain showed no abnormality that could have explained her symptoms. But that seemingly slight blow to her head presumably caused damage to the area in her brain responsible for ADH production. The damage is likely to be permanent.

I started her on twice-daily doses of ADH administered by nasal spray. Her urine output fell to normal, her thirst abated, and she returned to her normal lifestyle, freed from the worry of having to know the location of every accessible bathroom in town.

## Diet and nutrition

### SMOKING OUT THE OMEGA-3S

*Q I know that fish is a rich source of heart-healthy omega-3 fatty acids. Does smoking or pickling reduce the amount of omega-3s?*

A Yes, and it may pose health risks as well. For example, fresh salmon is high in omega-3s, but smoking reduces the amount by about 75 percent. Fresh herring is also high in those beneficial fats, but pickling apparently destroy about 30 percent of them. While that still makes pickled herring a relatively rich source of omega-3s, both pickling and smoking can deposit carcinogenic compounds on the treated food. Indeed, eating pickled or smoked foods several times a week or more has been linked to an increased risk of developing certain cancers. So while the occasional smoked or pickled snack shouldn't jeopardize your health, it's best not to eat them regularly.

### TO PEEL OR NOT TO PEEL

*Q Does eating fruit and vegetable skins provide nutritional benefits?*

A Yes, but there may be hazards, too. Skins tend to be fairly high in insoluble fiber, which can lower the risk of some digestive disorders, and they're loaded with phytonutrients, which may help prevent many diseases. But conventionally grown produce is usually coated with tiny amounts of pesticide residues. With certain items—apples, bell peppers, cucumbers, eggplants, peaches, pears, sweet potatoes, and tomatoes—the pesticides may be trapped under a layer of wax. Whether it's harmful to consume those residues is not clear. For maximum safety, particularly with children, you could scrub produce in a highly diluted solution of liquid dish detergent, which should remove most of the pesticides and wax. Or you could peel it—especially apples, peaches, and pears, which may be waxed and have particularly heavy residues. Alternatively, choose organically grown produce, which harbors very little or no residue. Organic produce should still be washed to remove other contaminants.

## ARE NONPOISONOUS MUSHROOMS HARMFUL?

*Q*  *I've heard that grocery-store mushrooms contain potentially harmful substances. Is that true?*

*A*  Yes, but the actual risks are vanishingly small. Mushrooms contain purines, which can aggravate gout, and agaritine, which causes kidney, liver, or stomach cancer in lab animals. But so many foods contain purines that it's impractical for gout sufferers to restrict their diet; instead, they're usually advised to take antigout drugs such as allopurinol *(Zyloprim)* or probenecid *(Benemid)*. And mushrooms contain only a trace of agaritine. While no studies have examined its effects on humans, researchers estimate that if 10,000 people ate a serving of raw mushrooms every day for 70 years, agaritine would cause only one case of cancer. Cooking lowers the agaritine content by about a third, further cutting that risk. Moreover, mushrooms are rich in chemicals that appear to fight breast cancer and, in theory, other cancers as well. And they're generally good sources of protein, B vitamins, and several minerals.

## ARE BANANAS BENEFICIAL?

**Q** *Your September story on phytochemicals in produce didn't mention bananas. Don't they contain any of those potentially disease-fighting compounds?*

**A** Yes, but less than the average amount in other fruits and vegetables. That's mainly because the major phytochemicals tend to be the same pigmented substances that give produce its color. Brightly colored foods such as blueberries and kale are loaded with phytochemicals—but bananas are not, because their flesh is relatively pale. However, bananas contain plenty of other worthwhile nutrients, notably vitamin B6, vitamin C, and potassium.

## THE POWER OF PULP

**Q** *I prefer to use a juicer and drink my vegetables. But I've heard that I'm throwing out nutrients with the pulp. Would it be healthier to blend some veggies and tomato juice together, and drink the slush, pulp and all?*

**A** Yes, though you might want to choose low-sodium tomato juice. Using a juicer is an easy way to reap most of the vitamins, minerals, and certain other disease-fighting substances from vegetables and fruits. But juicing strains out most of the fiber, some of the vitamins and minerals, and possibly other, unknown beneficial substances. In contrast, using a blender retains everything in the produce. Drinking slushed fruits or vegetables can be even healthier than eating them whole, since you're apt to consume more of them.

## DOES EGGPLANT PARMESAN COUNT?

**Q** *I love eggplant parmesan. But does it actually count as a serving of vegetables?*

**A** Yes—though it's not particularly healthful. The eggplant is usually salted, battered, and fried first, then topped with lots of tomato sauce and cheese. So a typical one-cup portion contains about 50 percent of your daily quota of artery-clogging saturated fat and 30 percent of your sodium. The eggplant itself contains only negligible amounts of vitamins, minerals, and fiber. Though the skin contains phytochemicals, or potentially disease-fighting substances, it's usually peeled off and discarded. The tomato sauce and cheese fortify the dish somewhat: The sauce is a good source of vitamins A and C as well as the antioxidant lycopene, which has been linked with a reduction in prostate-cancer risk. And the cheese is rich in calcium and protein.

## VEGGIES AND BLOOD CLOTS

**Q** *I take a daily aspirin to prevent blood clots. But I also enjoy eating collard greens, kale, and spinach, all rich in vitamin K, which promotes blood clotting. Do I need to quit eating these greens?*

**A** No. Leafy greens do contain ample amounts of clot-promoting vitamin K. So eating them could weaken the effects of certain anticlotting drugs such as warfarin *(Coumadin)*, but only if you suddenly started consuming huge amounts of them. In contrast, aspirin prevents clots in a totally different way that's not affected by vitamin K, so you can enjoy all the healthful greens you want.

## BAKED VS. SWEET POTATOES

**Q** *You said that regular potatoes have a very high glycemic load. Are sweet potatoes a healthier alternative?*

**A** Yes—but that doesn't mean you need to abandon regular potatoes. High-glycemic foods contain lots of easily digested carbohydrates that can rapidly raise blood sugar; some evidence suggests that a high-glycemic diet may increase the risk of heart disease and diabetes. A regular potato's glycemic load is very high, while a sweet potato's is roughly average. Moreover, sweet potatoes are higher in fiber and most nutrients than regular potatoes. Still, the regular kind of potato can add variety to your diet, as well as more folate than a sweet potato and moderate amounts of several other nutrients. So an occasional baked potato can still be a good nutritional choice, especially if the rest of your diet contains relatively few high-glycemic foods, notably sugar and refined flour.

## NUTRITIOUS COOKING

**Q** *What are the best ways to cook vegetables so they retain the most nutrients?*

**A** In a few cases, heating actually increases the availability of certain nutrients, such as the antioxidants in carrots, spinach, and tomatoes. But in general, heat and water can strip produce of valuable substances such as vitamin A, vitamin C, the B vitamins, and some phytochemicals, or potentially disease-fighting compounds.

That's why it's best to avoid boiling, which leaches nutrients into water that is then discarded. Stewing also draws beneficial substances into the cooking liquid, but they remain part of the stew. Baking, roasting, grilling, and frying typically don't use water but often do use oils, which add fat and calories. And the foods are exposed to higher temperatures for a longer time.

For the healthiest results, use a microwave, steamer, or pressure cooker, which all preserve nutrients about equally well.

## ARE RUNNY EGGS RISKY?

**Q** *I like poached eggs with yolks that aren't fully firm. Am I risking a salmonella infection?*

**A** Yes, but the risk is quite small. The Food and Drug Administration estimates that only 1 in 20,000 eggs contain salmonella bacteria. You can kill any bacteria and eliminate the slim chance of infection by cooking eggs till both the whites and yolks are firm. If you want runny yolks with no risk, look for pasteurized eggs, which are flash-heated to destroy any bacteria.

Salmonella poisoning causes fever, stomach cramps, and diarrhea that generally last about a week, occasionally requiring hospitalization. People with impaired immunity, pregnant women, infants, and older people are at increased risk of severe complications. So while other people can decide for themselves whether the risk warrants giving up runny yolks or unpasteurized eggs, high-risk individuals should take those precautions.

## VEGETABLES VS. FRUITS

**Q** *You recently told a reader who ate lots of fruit to add some veggies, too. My question is the opposite: I eat lots of vegetables but little fruit. Am I missing out nutritionally?*

**A** Probably not much, though eating a variety of both vegetables and fruit is still the best approach. Fruits tend to provide more soluble fiber, which helps lower cholesterol levels, than vegetables do. But while both food groups are generally rich in vitamins and minerals, vegetables tend to supply more B vitamins, calcium, iron, and phytochemicals, or potentially disease-fighting plant compounds. And while numerous studies have linked a high intake of either fruits or vegetables with reduced risks of hypertension, coronary heart disease, and cancer, vegetables appear to provide more protection against certain cancers than fruits do. So while adding fruit might make a vegetable-rich diet even more nutritious, the vegetables alone should already be providing ample nutritional benefits.

## DIGESTING FIBER

**Q** *In a recent issue you said fiber slows the digestion of food. But I thought fiber helped to protect against colon cancer by speeding up digestion. Which is true?*

**A** Fiber does slow digestion; however, it fights colon cancer by hastening the elimination of waste products. Some of the fiber you consume dissolves into a gel that slows the absorption of nutrients from the stomach and small intestine. That helps keep blood-sugar levels from spiking, which may help lower cardiovascular risk in susceptible people. Fiber can also discourage overeating by making you feel fuller. In contrast, the colon, or large intestine, plays only a limited role in the digestion of food but a major role in excretion. Fiber entering the colon helps create soft, bulky stools that speed the excretion of potentially cancer-causing wastes.

## PEANUT-BUTTER PERIL?

**Q** *Does the aflatoxin in peanut butter pose a significant health threat?*

**A** Almost certainly no. Aflatoxin, a chemical produced by mold that grows on various harvested nuts and grains, particularly peanuts, can cause cancer in lab animals. And human population studies in Africa and Asia have linked the toxin to increased risk of liver cancer. But the amounts of aflatoxin in foods over there are thousands of times higher than in the U.S.—and human studies in this country have found no liver-cancer link. If the small amount of aflatoxin in peanut butter does threaten the liver, the risk is almost surely extremely low. Even if you ate a peanut butter sandwich every day for 30 years, aflatoxin would still be less of a concern than the fat, salt, and sugar found in many peanut butter brands, according to John Groopman, Ph.D., a leading aflatoxin researcher and chairman of the department of environmental health sciences at Johns Hopkins University.

## SMOKED MEAT AND CANCER

**Q** *Can eating smoked meat or fish increase the risk of cancer?*

**A** Possibly. A few studies have found that consuming those foods a couple of times a week or more increases the risk of developing certain cancers. That's because the smoke from burning wood contains large amounts of carcinogenic carbon compounds. Such compounds are found in many smoke flavorings as well as in smoked foods. Further, the preservatives used in many smoked products may react with compounds in meat to form additional carcinogens. So while the occasional smoked snack shouldn't jeopardize your health, frequent consumption of such foods should be avoided.

## STALE PRODUCE

**Q** *Does the nutritional content of fruits and vegetables change after they're harvested?*

**A** The mineral content doesn't. But in most vegetables, the vitamins and phytochemicals—potentially disease-fighting substances—generally start breaking down after harvest. In fact, frozen vegetables can be more nutritious than "fresh" items that are no longer very fresh. In contrast, the vitamins and phytochemicals in foods that keep ripening after they're picked—including fruits as well as tomatoes, peppers, and avocados (which are technically fruits)—generally increase until they're fully ripe. And scientists have just learned that certain nutrients also increase in at least some fruits that don't ripen, such as berries and cherries, after the fruit has been harvested and refrigerated.

## COMPLETE PLANT PROTEINS

**Q** *I eat a lot of rice and beans, but I've heard that neither of them is a complete source of protein, since each is missing essential amino acids. How should I combine them to get enough complete protein?*

**A** Don't bother. If you're eating the recommended two to three servings of dairy plus a modest amount of meat each day, you're almost surely already getting enough protein. Even if you consume mainly plant proteins, trying to balance a few specific foods isn't necessary. Instead, eat a wide variety of legumes, nuts, seeds, grains, and vegetables throughout the day. That will supply your body with enough essential amino acids to manufacture the complete proteins that may be missing from individual items.

## FRUITS AND VEGETABLES

*Q  I know I should eat five to nine servings of fruits and vegetables every day. Would I get the same benefits from eating just fruit?*

**A** Not quite. It's true that fruits tend to pack more soluble fiber, the kind that helps lower cholesterol levels, and slightly more fiber overall than vegetables do. (Vegetables tend to be higher in insoluble fiber, which helps speed wastes through the colon.) And both fruits and vegetables are generally rich in vitamins and minerals. However, vegetables are more likely than fruits to be high in B vitamins, calcium, and iron. And vegetables tend to contain more phytochemicals, a vast array of plant compounds that theoretically may help protect against disease.

Many studies have linked a high intake of both fruits and vegetables with a reduced risk of hypertension, coronary heart disease, and cancer. But for some cancers, the evidence of protection is somewhat stronger for vegetables than for fruits. Ideally, eating a variety of vegetables as well as fruits is the best approach.

## MICROWAVE COOKING

*Q  Does microwave cooking cause any loss of nutrients or other unhealthful change?*

**A** Microwave cooking may actually retain nutrients better than traditional methods. That's because the longer you cook food, particularly in water that's discarded before eating, the more nutrients are lost. For example, one study found that spinach retained 100 percent of its folate—a water-soluble B vitamin—when cooked in a microwave, vs. 77 percent when stovetop boiled. Moreover, briefer cooking of meats produces lower levels of potentially cancer-causing chemicals.

But microwaving tends to heat foods unevenly, so the outer portions may not get hot enough. To help ensure germ-killing temperatures throughout, cover the food, leaving a hole for steam to escape. (Waxed paper is preferable to plastic wrap, which might transfer possibly harmful amounts of plastic to the food. For the same reason, use only containers labeled "microwave safe.") Stir and turn the food during cooking and let it stand for a while afterwards, as directed. And check its temperature in several places with a food thermometer.

---

## ONION EATERS

**Q** *Does eating onions provide me with any health benefits?*

**A** Green onions (such as scallions) have plenty of potassium and vitamins A and C. But most onions are very low in vitamins and minerals. However, like other "allium" vegetables—garlic, chives, leeks—all onions are rich in potentially disease-fighting substances, particularly sulfur compounds. Those compounds may help inhibit blood clots, reduce cholesterol levels, relax the arteries, and block the formation and effects of cancer-causing chemicals. Moreover, certain indigestible carbohydrates in onions, called oligosaccharides, may help speed the passage of cancer-causing substances through the colon. All those actions may help explain observational findings that link eating onions and other allium vegetables with reduced risks of colon and stomach cancer, lower cholesterol levels and blood pressure, and reduced risk of coronary heart disease. So in theory, eating onions and related vegetables may enhance your body's disease-fighting abilities.

## CANOLA-OIL CONCERNS

**Q** *I recently received an e-mail claiming that canola oil and its cousin, rapeseed oil, are toxic substances that can cause everything from asthma to heart disease. Is that true?*

**A** No. That widely circulating myth is based on the fact that up to 60 percent of the fatty acids in ordinary rapeseed oil (derived from the rape plant, a relative of mustard) is erucic acid; high concentrations of that substance can cause heart disease in animals. But canola oil is made from a type of rape plant specially bred to contain only a minuscule quantity of erucic acid. Studies in animals have found no ill effects from consuming such tiny amounts. In the only research involving humans that we could find—a small study of Chinese children whose main source of dietary fat was regular rapeseed oil—there were similarly no toxic effects.

Canola critics also claim that heating the oil can generate potentially cancer-causing fumes. But that happens only when it's heated so much that it emits thick black smoke—and canola is no different from other oils in that regard. Of course, canola is not just safe: It's also one of the most healthful oils, since it's low in artery-clogging saturated fat and relatively high in monounsaturated fat, omega-3 fatty acids, and vitamin E, all of which may be good for the heart.

## BEST BITS OF BROCCOLI

**Q** *What is the most nutritious part of the broccoli plant?*

**A** The florets contain substantially more cancer-fighting phytochemicals and beta-carotene (a precursor of vitamin A) than the stalks, and about the same amounts of minerals and vitamin C. Whether you're eating the florets or the stalks, broccoli that's raw or lightly cooked (by microwaving or steaming) will supply the most nutrients. For a healthy sandwich or salad topping, look for broccoli sprouts, which pack 20 to 50 times more phytochemicals than the full-grown plant and comparable amounts of vitamins and minerals.

## A MORE NUTRITIOUS CHEESE?

**Q** *Are there any nutritional differences between soft and hard cheeses?*

**A** Ounce for ounce, hard cheeses tend to offer a better nutritional profile than soft cheeses. That's mainly because cheese loses moisture as it ages and hardens. So each serving of the harder types generally packs more calcium, protein, and minerals than the softer, younger types. Moreover, the harder, aged ones—excluding grating cheeses like Parmesan—tend to contain less sodium, because they're generally more flavorful, so less salt is needed to enhance their taste. There's no consistent connection between firmness and fat content. However, lower-fat versions of virtually any cheese typically provide 25 to 50 percent less fat than the regular versions and at least as much of the beneficial nutrients.

## DRIED-FRUIT FACTS

**Q** *How do dried fruits stack up nutritionally against fresh ones?*

**A** Better in some ways, worse in others. Reducing the water content of fruit concentrates its fiber and minerals, certain vitamins (notably vitamin A), and many phytochemicals, potentially disease-fighting substances found in plants. But the sugar and calorie contents rise by comparable amounts. Moreover, drying destroys the water-soluble vitamins, including C and the B vitamins, as well as certain heat-sensitive phytochemicals. So while dried fruits can supply a lot of certain nutrients, a balanced daily diet should include at least some fresh fruits plus a few servings of vegetables. (Note that dried fruits treated with sulfites retain more of their color, vitamins, and phytochemicals than untreated fruits, but they can cause allergic reactions or asthma attacks in susceptible individuals.)

---

## LEAFY GREENS AND BLOOD CLOTS

**Q** *I was recently prescribed warfarin* (Coumadin) *for the prevention of blood clots. My doctor warned me to remove leafy green vegetables such as lettuce, brussels sprouts, cabbage, and broccoli from my diet. Is it really necessary for me to avoid such nutritious foods?*

**A** No. It's true that leafy green vegetables contain vitamin K, which tends to counteract the anticlotting actions of warfarin. So in theory, eating lots of leafy greens might make warfarin less effective—but only to a relatively small extent. And that effect shouldn't matter at all, since the warfarin dose should be adjusted regularly, based on your blood-clotting time while you're on your usual diet, including whatever amount of leafy greens you habitually eat. The only precaution you need to follow is that you shouldn't drastically change your intake of leafy greens—or any other part of your diet—while you're on warfarin, since that conceivably could alter your clotting time and, in turn, your need for the drug.

## MUST EVERY MEAL BE BALANCED?

**Q** *For several years, I've conscientiously tried to eat a healthy balanced diet every day. Now I read that for best results, every meal must be balanced. Is that true?*

**A** No. Your body has enough reserves of various nutrients to thrive for a while if some meals are unbalanced, or even missed. For example, foods that provide energy—protein, carbohydrates, and fats—should be replenished daily. Water-soluble vitamins, including the B-complex vitamins and vitamin C, will last two to three days. Your body stores enough minerals and fat-soluble vitamins, such as A, D, and E, to last weeks or even months.

## DIGESTING SOYBEANS

**Q** *I can no longer eat beans because they give me gas and intestinal cramps. If I eat tofu, will I have the same problems?*

**A** Processed soy products such as tofu are less likely to cause intestinal discomfort. Soybeans and other legumes contain carbohydrates called oligosaccharides, which the body can't digest since it lacks the necessary enzyme, alpha-galactosidase. So the intact oligosaccharides move on to the lower intestine, where they're broken down by bacteria, producing gas. The processing of soy products such as tofu, tempeh, miso, and soy "protein isolate" removes the oligosaccharides; all of these products are easier to digest than whole soybeans. You can eliminate most oligosaccharides from raw beans by soaking them overnight. You might also try *Beano,* a product that provides the missing enzyme. (People with diabetes should check with their doctor before taking Beano, since the enzyme produces a type of sugar that might hinder their blood-sugar control.)

## ARE SOY NUTS REALLY NUTS?

**Q** *A recent issue recommends nuts as a heart-healthy snack food. Does that suggestion include soy nuts as well?*

**A** Yes, we heartily recommend filling your nut dish with soy nuts. However, soy "nuts" are actually roasted soybeans—a type of legume. Like actual nuts, soy nuts are rich in nutrients, including protein, vitamin E, potassium, and fiber, that may help reduce the risk of coronary heart disease. At about 130 calories per 1-ounce serving, soy nuts contain roughly 25 percent fewer calories and significantly less total and saturated fat than an equivalent serving of peanuts (another legume) or real nuts such as almonds, cashews, and walnuts. Recently, the Food and Drug Administration concluded that 25 grams a day of soy protein (found in soy nuts and other foods made with soybeans), combined with a diet low in saturated fat and cholesterol, may help reduce the risk of coronary heart disease by lowering blood-cholesterol levels. Soybean-based foods that meet certain FDA requirements can now include that health claim on their label. (A quarter-cup serving of soy nuts contains a little more than 8 grams of soy protein.)

## YAMS VS. SWEET POTATOES

*What's the difference between yams and sweet potatoes? And do all yams and sweet potatoes have "natural estrogen"?*

In the U.S. some people use the word "yam" to describe the moister, sweeter, orange-fleshed variety of the familiar Thanksgiving root and reserve "sweet potato" for the drier, yellow-fleshed version. But most people use the terms interchangeably. Both varieties provide loads of carotenoids (many of which are precursors of vitamin A) plus a good supply of vitamin C, fiber, protein, calcium, magnesium, and potassium.

However, neither variety bears any relation to "true" yams, which are much larger roots—generally at least 18 inches long, sometimes much larger—commonly eaten in Africa, Asia, and the Caribbean, but usually available here only in specialty markets. True yams are low in carotenoids but are otherwise just as nutritious as sweet potatoes.

At least one type of true yam—the Mexican wild yam—contains chemicals that the body converts into the female hormones estrogen and progesterone. Limited research suggests that American yams and sweet potatoes probably have at most only a small amount of those chemicals. Mexican wild yam is used in some "natural estrogen" or "phytoestrogen" supplements.

## TYPES OF FIBER

*A recent issue provided an interesting and useful article on fiber. Could you expand on the respective roles and importance of soluble vs. insoluble fiber?*

Many foods contain both types of fiber: soluble fiber, which dissolves in water, and insoluble fiber, which does not. The two types of fiber behave very differently inside your digestive tract. Soluble fiber, plentiful in beans, oats, some vegetables, and most fruits and whole grains, takes on a gelatinous consistency that will make you feel fuller and less inclined to overeat; it also helps to lower insulin and cholesterol levels. Insoluble fiber, found in whole grains, beans, most vegetables, and some fruits, absorbs water, making stools softer and bulkier. In theory at least, that may reduce the risk of colon cancer by speeding potentially cancer-causing wastes through the colon and also reducing their concentrations.

## Doctors

### WHAT DOES A D.O. DO?

**Q** *Can you tell me what the difference is between a D.O. and an M.D.?*

**A** D.O. (doctor of osteopathy) receives a medical education that's basically equivalent to that of an M.D. (doctor of medicine). Osteopaths are trained and licensed to perform all aspects of traditional medical care—including diagnosis, drug prescription, and surgery. In fact, they can specialize in virtually any area of medicine, although most choose primary care.

The difference between the two degrees is that osteopaths are also trained in osteopathic medicine, which emphasizes how the musculoskeletal system, particularly the spine, affects the entire body. They diagnose and treat certain conditions by manipulating joints. That can mean stretching the wrist of someone with carpal-tunnel syndrome or manipulating the spine to treat low-back pain, for example. Some osteopaths also use such therapy along with conventional treatments to ease the discomfort of conditions such as asthma, migraine, and pneumonia.

---

## ✚ *Office* **Visit**

# YOUR SYMPTOMS: SAY WHAT YOU MEAN

HIS PROBLEM WAS PERSISTENT daily headaches that began the previous winter as soon as the weather turned cold. At about that time, this 37-year-old systems analyst had taken a faster-paced, better-paying job that he hoped would enable him to buy a home and replace the 20-year-old jalopy he had to drive an hour each way to and from work. After a workup that included a referral to a neurologist, CT scans and MRIs of his head and neck, and a complete laboratory survey, his doctors decided the long commute and increased job stress were causing tension headaches. But *Valium* and several muscle relaxants didn't help. Some well-meaning friends suggested he get psychiatric help. He remained miserable.

When I questioned him closely, I learned that his headaches waned noticeably several hours after he arrived at work and returned soon after he got home in the evening, yet they never bothered him on weekends. Those details gave me a hunch. I asked him to drive straight to my office after work one evening. He arrived with a splitting headache. A blood test showed an elevated level of carboxy hemoglobin, an indicator of carbon-monoxide poisoning. He got rid of that car so fast that we never found out the source of the exhaust leak that nearly cost him his life. His headaches disappeared just as fast.

## COMMUNICATE YOUR CONDITION

For many people the notion of modern medical diagnosis con-
jures up images of assorted high-tech tests, computer analyses,
and complex imaging equipment. All these tools do help enor-
mously in diagnosing disease, yet none is more important than
the patient's ability to explain his or her case to the doctor.
Inadequately expressed symptoms can lead even good physicians
down the garden path to misdiagnosis. If you do your part by
communicating your symptoms accurately and forcefully, your
doctor stands the best chance of getting to the bottom of your
problem. Here's how:

• Get the timeline right. Take along a written list of all of your
complaints and do your best to list them in chronological order.
Knowing which symptoms came first can often be the decisive
factor in arriving at a workable diagnosis—as it was with the systems analyst's headaches.

• Get down to business quickly. Time-stressed doctors have a
tendency to narrow down the list of possible diagnoses fairly
quickly after an office visit begins. You need to make your concerns known at the outset before your physician jumps to what
may turn out to be an erroneous conclusion.

• Be specific. Instead of complaining vaguely about pain, rate
it on a scale of zero to 10 (with 10 being the worst). Describe the
quality of the pain. Is it dull and aching as with tooth pain? Does
your chest feel on fire, as with heartburn? Does the pain sting like
an insect bite? Or is it a painful pressure, as if an elephant were
sitting on your chest? Does the pain radiate or spread into adjacent areas? How long has it hurt, and how often does it hurt? Do
changes in your position, exercise, sexual activity, or emotional
state affect the pain? Does anything make it feel better? Or
worse?

• If you fear the worst, say so. If you dismiss abdominal pain
as "probably just gas," your doctor may be tempted to agree—

even if you're secretly worried about ovarian cancer. I once saw a patient who had undergone six months of psychiatric treatment for a presumed anxiety syndrome. Numerous tests seeking a physical cause for her lightheadedness, sweating, and shakiness had come up negative. Careful questioning revealed that her symptoms kicked in only when her heart skipped a beat or two. Once I reassured her that the occasional missed beats were normal, the symptoms disappeared.

- Practice full disclosure. Be sure to tell your physician about visits to other doctors or specialists. Different specialists, each scrutinizing seemingly unrelated symptoms, can miss the forest for the trees. A recent example is a 43-year-old woman who saw a cardiologist for her high blood pressure, an orthopedist for her backaches, an internist for her diabetes, and a neurologist for her headaches. It turned out that all those problems stemmed from a single cause—a pituitary tumor causing Cushing's disease, an uncommon disorder that in turn caused her adrenal glands to produce too much cortisol. That potentially fatal condition had gone undiagnosed—and untreated—for nearly five years because this patient had not discussed all her symptoms thoroughly with any one physician. When she finally got around to doing so, her combination of symptoms prompted appropriate testing—and an eventual cure.

## Ear problems

### SWAB OUT EAR WAX?

**Q** *I use cotton swabs to clean wax out of my ears. But the box label warns me not to. What's the harm?*

**A** Swabbing out the wax can irritate or injure the delicate lining of the ear canal, causing itchiness or bleeding and increasing the risk of ear infection. If you have lots of wax, swabs can push it deeper into the ear canal, where it compacts and hardens. That can cause hearing loss, dizziness, or pain. Moreover, poking anything into your ear canal can damage the eardrum. Actually, most people don't need to clean out the wax, which gradually works its way out of the ear on its own. If it does become necessary to remove it, use ear drops such as carbamide peroxide *(Debrox Drops, E.R.O. Drops)*, or try the following home recipe: Mix half a teaspoon of baking soda in 2 ounces of warm water and pour into a dropper bottle. Use a few drops twice a day for up to a week, and discard any leftover solution. (Don't use ear drops if you have a perforated eardrum or are prone to ear infections.)

### RINGING EARS

**Q** *For two years, I've had constant ringing in my ear that's gradually getting stronger. Tests by an ear specialist were inconclusive. What's going on, and what can I do about it?*

**A** The cause of ringing or other noise in the ear, called tinnitus, often can't be determined. Tinnitus can result from almost any ear disorder, such as impacted earwax or infection. It can also be a symptom of anemia, cardiovascular disease, or Ménière's disease. Tinnitus is often associated with hearing loss.

Treating the underlying disorder, if one can be found, may stop the noise. If not, you can cover up the noise by playing background music or by using a tinnitus masker, which is worn like a hearing aid and makes a whining sound. Alcohol, caffeine, nicotine, and loud noises may aggravate tinnitus in some people.

## EAR OF FLYING

**Q** *Whenever I fly, I chew gum and yawn on both ascent and descent. Still, I experience pain in my ears, especially on descent. Afterward, my ears feel "blocked" for the rest of the day. Is there anything I can do about this?*

**A** Your problem probably stems from congestion blocking the eustachian tube, which connects your nose and middle ear. When that happens, the change in cabin pressure during takeoff and landing can make the eardrum retract or expand, causing pain and impairing hearing. To keep the eustachian tube open, try taking a decongestant—preferably a short-acting nasal spray or drops, such as phenylephrine 0.5% *(Neo-Synephrine)*—shortly before takeoff. A second dose may be needed shortly before landing.

## MÉNIÈRE'S DISEASE

**Q** *What can you tell me about Ménière's disease? My doctor says there's no treatment. Is that true?*

**A** The cause of Ménière's disease, a disorder that affects the inner ear, is unknown. Symptoms include vertigo (a spinning sensation) and tinnitus (ringing or other noise) in one ear or occasionally both ears. Gradual hearing loss often occurs. An ear, nose, and throat specialist can confirm the diagnosis with tests of balance and hearing. To rule out an acoustic neuroma—a benign tumor that can cause symptoms similar to those of Ménière's disease—a computerized tomography (CT) scan or magnetic resonance image (MRI) of the internal auditory canal within the skull should be done. Treatment of Ménière's disease is usually not very effective. Strategies include diet therapy (usually low-sodium) and certain medications (antihistamines, sedatives, or diuretics). As a last resort, part of the inner ear may have to be surgically destroyed to provide relief.

## LABYRINTHITIS

**Q** *Several months ago, I experienced dizziness so severe that I couldn't walk or even open my eyes. I was rushed to a hospital, where the problem was diagnosed as labyrinthitis and treated with* Antivert. *Four months later I still sometimes feel light-headed and have trouble keeping my balance when I look back over my shoulder. Will this go on forever?*

**A** Probably not. Usually, each succeeding attack gets shorter and milder, although some people continue to have dizzy spells at irregular intervals for many years.

Labyrinthitis is an inflammation of the maze of inner-ear canals that control balance. The disorder usually arises from nasal congestion caused by a cold or allergy. The result is vertigo, a spinning sensation that disrupts balance. Certain medications may help control the dizziness. These drugs include dimenhydrinate, sold over the counter as *Dramamine,* and meclizine, available by prescription as *Antivert* or over the counter as *Bonine* or *Dramamine II.*

# Enzyme disorders

## GAUCHER DISEASE: PRICEY BUT EFFECTIVE THERAPY

**Q** *I am 70 years old and have been diagnosed with Gaucher disease. My platelet and white-cell counts have diminished. My doctor doesn't give me anything for it and only checks my blood count. Can you suggest something I can do for it?*

**A** You should strongly consider seeing a Gaucher-disease specialist who can do a more thorough evaluation and decide whether you might benefit from drug therapy. Gaucher disease is an inherited enzyme deficiency that can cause many complications, including bone deterioration, bone and joint pain, liver and spleen enlargement, anemia, and an inability to produce white blood cells and platelets. Long-term enzyme replacement therapy with imiglucerase *(Cerezyme)* now offers a generally safe and effective way to control and even reverse those complications. *Cerezyme* is administered intravenously, usually every two weeks. The drug's biggest drawback is its staggering cost: $170,000 per year, on average. *Cerezyme* is covered by Medicare and private insurers, though private coverage may include a lifetime cap. For the name of a specialist in your area and for more information about the disease, contact the National Gaucher Foundation (800-GAUCHER, 800-428-2437; *www.gaucherdisease.org).*

# Eye care

## FLASHBULB SAFETY

**Q** *Can flash photography injure a newborn baby's eyes?*

**A** No. Camera-light flashes last only a fraction of a second. That's too little time to damage anyone's eyes, even if he or she is looking right at the flash or having multiple photos taken. Further, the eyes can adjust rapidly to greater changes in light intensity, such as stepping from a dark room into full sunlight. Our consultants say that no special precautions are needed when photographing newborns.

## COMPUTER-VISION SYNDROME

**Q** *I spend most days working at a computer. Lately it looks as if there are more red blood vessels in the whites of my eyes. Is that normal?*

**A** Yes. The strain of prolonged staring at a computer monitor can cause those blood vessels to become engorged, creating the illusion that new ones have appeared. Your eyes may also feel dry and itchy. Resting, drinking plenty of water, and reducing eyestrain should resolve the problem. (Consult an ophthalmologist if the symptoms persist.) Here's how to help prevent the problem from recurring:
- Give your eyes regular breaks. And try to blink frequently, to distribute moisture to your corneas.
- Reduce glare by adjusting the surrounding light and the

screen contrast or by using a screen filter. Keep the top of your monitor at or just below eye level, and keep your eyes at the same distance from the screen as you would from a book.

- Be sure that eyeglasses or contacts fit well and are the correct prescription.
- Consider buying either a liquid-crystal-display (LCD) monitor or a regular monitor with a high "refresh rate," both of which ease eyestrain by flickering less than other monitors.

## EYELID CHOLESTEROL DEPOSITS

**Q** *I have cholesterol deposits in my eyelids. What causes them and how can I get rid of them?*

**A** These bumps form when surplus cholesterol in the blood collects under the skin surrounding the eyes. While they usually appear spontaneously for no apparent reason, they can also be a warning sign of high cholesterol levels, so you should have your levels checked. Regardless of the cause, the deposits are not harmful. But if they bother you, you can have them removed by a simple surgical procedure.

## SPOTS BEFORE YOUR EYES

**Q** *My husband, who is 69 years old, has a large gray floater in his left eye. Are there any medications or herbs that will dissolve the floater, or is there an operation that can remove it?*

**A** No. Floaters are tiny condensations in the vitreous, the jelly-like substance inside the eye; they appear as tiny clumps or strands that float in the field of vision. The most common cause of floaters is the aging process, which can cause the vitreous to shrink and pull away from the retina, the light-sensitive layer at the back of the eye. A blow to the head can also separate the vitreous from the retina, allowing the unanchored jelly to shrink. While some floaters last for years, many fade with time and become more tolerable. Your husband could try repeatedly moving his eyes around, to shake up the vitreous and possibly push the floater out of his field of vision. Note that in rare cases the retina may tear as the vitreous pulls away. So anyone who experiences a sudden increase in the number of floaters, particularly if they're accompanied by sudden flashes of light, should see an ophthalmologist.

## TWITCHING EYELID

**Q** *I have a fluttering eyelid, which I cannot control. It flutters several times a day for 10 to 20 seconds. What causes this, and is there anything I can do to stop it?*

**A** No one knows for sure what causes twitching of the eyelid. Some doctors believe that rest and stress reduction may help. Sometimes pressing on the twitchy area for a few seconds provides temporary relief. If it hasn't gone away after three or four weeks, though, consult an eye-care specialist. If a thorough examination uncovers no underlying cause and the twitching is particularly severe and persistent, you may want to ask about the possibility of injecting botulinum toxin *(Botox)* to certain muscles around the eyes to stop the twitching. There are risks, however, since *Botox* is a drug that temporarily paralyzes muscles. And some doctors think that would be overkill for patients with chronic, unremitting eyelid spasms.

## EASY ON THE EYES

**Q** *Are computer monitors with LCD screens really better for the eyes than regular monitors?*

**A** Most desktop monitors sold today contain a cathode-ray tube (CRT) that flickers; some screens may flicker enough to cause eyestrain in a few individuals, whether or not they can actually see the flickering. Liquid-crystal-display (LCD) monitors don't flicker at all. (They also use less power than CRT types, and their flat screens take up much less room.) But if you're experiencing eyestrain you could consider switching to a superior-quality CRT monitor with a high "refresh rate" (17- and 19-inch monitors can generally be used comfortably with a refresh rate of 75 Hz, but 85 Hz is preferable). Even a high-end CRT monitor will cost substantially less than an LCD, and it won't produce significant flickering.

## CONTACT-LENS INFECTIONS?

**Q** *I recently read that keeping extended-wear contact lenses in place overnight leads to increased risk of infection. I have been keeping my lenses in for a week at a time. Is that unsafe?*

**A** It may be. Extended-wear contact lens users are 10 to 15 times more likely than daily-wear users to develop corneal ulcers, which can become infected. In general, the risk increases with the length of time you wear your lenses, beginning with the first night's use. It is much safer to remove contact lenses daily, then clean and sterilize them each night.

## OFF-THE-RACK GLASSES

**Q** *Now that I'm over 40, is there any reason why I shouldn't use ready-to-wear reading glasses?*

**A** Go right ahead, if they're comfortable. Store-bought reading glasses are perfectly safe—and they're quite inexpensive. Such glasses work fine for most people with presbyopia (far-sightedness due to aging eyes). However, you may need to switch to customized prescription lenses if you notice signs of eyestrain, such as headaches or tired eyes. Be sure to have an eye examination every two years or so after age 45 to ensure that your eyes stay healthy.

## PLASTIC SUNGLASSES

**Q** *I've read that even clear plastic sunglass lenses block most ultraviolet light. Does that mean that my clear plastic prescription eyeglasses provide all the UV protection I need?*

**A** Probably. Only people who are at high risk of developing eye damage need to wear lenses with a special coating that blocks additional ultraviolet light. This includes people who spend large amounts of time in the sun; those who have had cataracts removed without the insertion of an artificial lens; and those who take certain medications, such as allopurinol *(Lopurin, Zyloprim),* phenothiazine compounds *(Compazine, Thorazine),* psoralen drugs *(Oxsoralen-Ultra, Trisoralen),* tretinoin *(Renova, Retin-A),* or the antibiotics doxycycline or tetracycline.

# SELF-HELP FOR IRRITATED EYES

WITH R. LINSY FARRIS, M.D., M.P.H.

**MY NEW PATIENT, AN ART DEALER,** came to see me after enduring two years of dry, burning, itching eyes. The condition had appeared suddenly while she was driving home from her 50th birthday party. Treatments prescribed by several specialists had helped only a little; her eyes still felt uncomfortable, her vision was blurred, and the artificial tears she was using caused her eye makeup to run down her face.

The thin, complex film of tears, mucus, and oils that covers the cornea, the transparent tissue in front of the iris, plays a critical role in keeping the eye comfortable and capable of admitting undistorted light rays. Trying to see clearly through a cornea with dry spots is like looking through a dirty, splotchy windshield.

## CAUSES OF DRY EYE

Although an inadequate production of tears seems the obvious cause of dry eye, in fact that's the problem in only 5 to 10 percent of all dry-eye patients. Aging was once thought to reduce the output of the tear glands, but this has been called into question.

Certain uncommon systemic conditions such as Sjogren's syndrome, an autoimmune disorder, are known to slow down tear production, but, more often, dry eye stems from a combination of disruption and excessive evaporation of the tear film. That can be caused by overly dry indoor air, contact-lens overuse, or staring at a computer too long without blinking. (Blinking replenishes and spreads tears across the cornea.)

The most common cause of dry eye, however, is, simply, dirty eyelids. Airborne dust, debris, and eye makeup can work onto the lid margins, the narrow strips of skin between the base of the eyelashes and the eyeball, and from there get into the tear film and impair its function. The upward-facing lower-lid margin can get especially untidy; under magnification, it looks like a dusty city apartment window ledge.

## WHAT DOES—AND DOESN'T—HELP

Like many dry-eye sufferers, my new patient found that the treatments she was prescribed not only didn't help, but in some cases made her eyes feel worse. Artificial tears didn't give her much relief. A stronger ointment prescribed for bedtime use gave her blurry vision in the morning. The allergy drops one doctor prescribed burned intolerably. After a corneal specialist inserted plugs in the tear ducts of her lower lids so the tears would not drain away as quickly, her eyes watered so much that tears ran down her cheeks.

In fact, the only thing these treatments accomplished was to further disrupt her natural tear layer by diluting and rinsing it away, much as the skin dries out when one takes several showers in the same day.

My initial advice to dry-eye patients is to make sure their living environment is kept at a minimum of 50 percent humidity. In our Northeastern climate, that usually means installing a humidifier for the dry winter months.

I also instruct women to choose only waterproof eye makeup, to apply mascara only to the tips of the upper eyelashes, and to refrain from using any makeup on the lower lids or lashes.

But the mainstay of treatment is a twice-daily routine of eyelid cleansing. The upper lids and lashes should be gently washed with a soft washcloth and warm water. To clean the all-important lower lid without rubbing the sensitive cornea, start with a 30-second warm-water compress to dissolve the oily deposits on the lid margin. Then pull the lid away from the eye and gently wipe the margin with a dry, tightly wound cotton-tipped applicator. In addition to cleaning the lid, this wipe massages tiny glands in the eyelid that release a small amount of oil into the tear layer to retard evaporation. The stimulation also produces reflex tearing.

If patients still suffer from dryness, I allow them to use artificial tears no more than four times a day. I recommend the single-use packets because they don't contain preservatives, which themselves can trigger allergic reactions.

The small number of patients for whom these measures don't bring full relief generally turn out to have allergies, which can be treated with appropriate drugs. The few who are truly deficient in tear production can be helped with special spectacles that trap moisture around the eye.

As for my patient, a new home humidifier, along with conscientious twice-a-day cleaning of her eyelids and lashes, soon enabled her to dispense almost entirely with artificial tears. A prescription eye drop helped clear up the seasonal allergic reaction that also turned out to be contributing to her problem.

## Fitness

### MORE SWEAT, MORE GAIN?

**Q** *If I make myself sweat more during exercise, by turning up the heat or wearing more clothes, will I get more benefits?*

**A** Possibly, but it's not worth the risks. Exercising in a hot setting increases not only sweating but also heart rate and oxygen consumption. That increases aerobic benefits, burns more calories, and causes some immediate weight loss. But the steps you mention aren't recommended because they can prevent sweat from evaporating and thus cooling the body; that in turn might lead to muscle cramps, dizziness, dehydration, or heatstroke. And those rapidly lost pounds are almost entirely water; they'll return once you drink enough to replenish the lost fluids.

Advocates of forced sweating claim one other benefit: It removes waste products from your system and flushes impurities from the skin's pores. However, both effects are minor; normal bathing cleanses the pores better than sweating, and urinating eliminates far more of the other wastes.

### MOTIONLESS MUSCLE GAIN?

**Q** *I've seen several ads for "no-work" exercise machines that stimulate muscles with electrical impulses. Can such devices help people bulk up or slim down?*

**A** No. The repeated shocks force rapid contractions, which can stimulate the growth of muscle fibers. But any gains are generally minuscule; even the best units, used to rehabilitate injured people, do little more than partially prevent muscle atrophy. Without regular exercise, electrical stimulation won't noticeably boost muscle size or strength, or burn enough calories to cause meaningful weight loss. And results from units like those you've seen advertised may be even more disappointing. A study of one popular model found that stimulating the major muscles of the arms, legs, and abdomen for 45 minutes three times a week for two months did not significantly change the participants' strength, weight, body fat, or overall appearance.

## FITNESS VS. FATNESS

**Q** *I am attempting to better understand how to interpret the Body Mass Index (BMI). For example, suppose there are identical twin brothers, each 5 feet 11 inches tall and with the same body frame. One is a couch potato and weighs 178 pounds. The other is an athlete who engages in regular aerobic activity and weight training and weighs 185 pounds. The first twin, who is demonstrably less healthy, would have a BMI of 24.9 and be labeled "normal weight," according to current standards. The second twin, who is much healthier, would have a BMI of 25.9 and be labeled "overweight." Comment?*

**A** While BMI is a useful general weight guideline, it can be misleading when applied to an individual without considering other important attributes of wellness. Your first twin's sedentary lifestyle puts him at increased risk for cardiovascular disease despite his "normal" BMI. If your second twin is truly fit, with low body fat and high aerobic capacity, he has no reason for concern despite his slightly "overweight" BMI. The extra weight is probably just healthy muscle.

## TIMING MEALS AND WORKOUTS

**Q** *Is it true that I'll get the maximum health benefit if I both exercise and eat my biggest meal in the morning?*

**A** That depends. For weight loss, morning workouts may be somewhat better. Some evidence suggests that exercising before breakfast burns more fat than later workouts, which are fueled mainly by proteins and carbohydrates from the day's earlier meals. (If you have heart disease, however, morning workouts may slightly increase your risk of heart attack.) Afternoons are probably better for building strength and endurance, since aerobic capacity, muscle strength, flexibility, coordination, and reaction time all peak between 4 and 7 p.m. But the most important consideration is just to find a workout time that you enjoy, since that will help you make exercise a regular habit. As for your biggest meal, the timing doesn't really matter, with one exception: Stuffing yourself shortly before bedtime can lead to poorer sleep, since the body is still working hard to digest the food.

## WHAT'S "PHYSICALLY FIT"?

**Q** *In a recent article you use the undefined term "physically fit." What does that mean?*

**A** It generally refers to cardiovascular fitness, or how effectively the heart and lungs supply oxygen to the muscles. While such fitness allows you to exercise longer—or just run for a bus without getting winded—its most important benefit is a reduced risk of major diseases such as coronary heart disease and stroke. Researchers evaluate cardiovascular fitness by measuring the heart rate during and after treadmill exercise. As a self-test, see how fast you can walk a mile without getting winded. That should take no more than about 18 minutes for moderately fit women in their 30s or 40s; the maximum for comparable men is about half a minute less. If you're past your 40s, allow an extra 30 seconds for each additional decade.

## BEST EXERCISE FOR FAT LOSS

**Q** *I've heard that in order to burn fat you must exercise moderately for at least 40 minutes, and that vigorous exercise burns sugar but not fat. Does that mean I should avoid high-intensity workouts if I want to lose weight?*

**A** Not necessarily. It's true that the body burns more fat than sugar during prolonged, easy-to-moderate exercise, but uses mainly sugar during hard exercise. However, researchers have not determined whether that physiological difference in fuel consumption translates into any meaningful difference in the amount of fat or weight you'd lose. What they do know is that you'll shed both fat and pounds if you consistently burn more calories than you take in from food. And the average person can do moderate exercise, such as brisk walking, for a much longer time than a vigorous one like running—and therefore burn significantly more calories overall. However, harder exercise can help you shed pounds if you use a special technique called interval training, in which you weave short bursts of vigorous exercise into a session of easier activity. Because the bursts generally don't cause much fatigue, you should still be able to exercise for a long time, and thus burn even more calories than if you stuck with a moderate pace only.

## AEROBIC EXERCISE

**Q** *Exactly what is it that makes an exercise "aerobic"?*

**A** During aerobic exercises such as swimming, jogging, and cycling, the muscles demand a continuous supply of oxygen to burn the energy stored in their cells. That forces the body to improve its ability to use oxygen; this eventually benefits the lungs and heart by increasing the efficiency of breathing and pumping oxygenated blood. Strength-training exercise, on the other hand, is usually nonaerobic; that is, the muscles derive energy from biochemical reactions that don't depend on oxygen. However, such exercise is equally important and has complementary benefits.

## AEROBIC CRAMPING

**Q** *About 15 minutes into my aerobics class, my calves begin to cramp. Why does that happen, and how can I prevent it?*

**A** Aerobic exercises, especially those that involve bouncing, tend to overwork the large muscle in the calf. The cramping problem might be avoided if you varied your exercise routine to stress different muscle groups.

Always be sure to stretch your calves before and after exercising: Stand about two feet from a wall and place your hands against it. Bend one knee and move the other leg out behind you, keeping that heel on the floor. Lean forward until you feel the stretch in your calf. Hold that position for 30 seconds, then repeat with the opposite leg. You can also help prevent cramps by drinking plenty of water both before and during strenuous workouts.

## RESTING HEART RATE I

Q *What is considered a "healthy" resting heart rate for a 47-year-old man, and how much can an exercise program lower that rate?*

A A normal resting heart rate varies from person to person but is usually between 60 and 80 beats per minute, regardless of age or gender. With exercise and proper aerobic conditioning, however, the resting heart rate can be between 50 and 60 beats per minute. Highly trained athletes can have a resting heart rate as low as 40 beats per minute.

## RESTING HEART RATE II

Q *I've heard that your resting heart rate indicates how aerobically fit you are, and that a rate below average means you're in good shape. But when should you take your pulse to determine that rate? Mine normally ranges from the upper 50s after waking to the mid-60s later in the day. When I'm tense and under pressure, my heart rate can soar into the upper 80s. Which of these is my resting heart rate?*

A The best time to determine your resting heart rate is before you get out of bed in the morning (unless you had a nightmare, which could make your pulse race). The resting heart rate for a well-conditioned adult is between 50 and 60 beats per minute. So your waking rate in the upper 50s is admirable. However, a heart rate lower than 50 in anyone other than a highly trained athlete could be caused by a problem involving the internal rhythmicity of the heart and should be checked.

## REDUCING RESISTANCE

**Q** *A while back, you said that people get the maximum benefit from strength training by repeating a particular maneuver until they're too tired to do even one more repetition. I'm 74 years old. Is straining that hard appropriate for someone my age?*

**A** No. People younger than ages 50 to 60 (depending on their strength and health) should indeed pick a weight or other resistance that temporarily exhausts the involved muscles after 8 to 12 repetitions. But older individuals should reduce the resistance and do 10 to 15 reps. Moreover, they should stop when the exercise starts to feel somewhat hard but not very hard. (When you can exceed 15 reps without struggling, increase the load by about 5 percent.) Those precautions are needed because older people are more susceptible to muscle strains, joint injuries, and heart problems. While that lower-intensity regimen will yield somewhat smaller muscle gains, studies have shown that it can still reduce premature mortality by up to 50 percent.

## SWIMMING FOR STRENGTH

**Q** *I swim a mile six days a week. I don't kick as hard as I'd like when swimming because it makes my back ache, so I exercise my legs by walking 5 miles once a week. Is this an adequate workout for upper- and lower-body strength?*

**A** The swimming gives your upper body a terrific workout. It tends to do less for your legs, especially if you don't work them hard. You might want to balance your upper- and lower-body workouts by swimming one day and walking the next.

## ROWING MACHINES

**Q** *What are the benefits of exercising on a rowing machine?*

**A** This is one of the best ways to exercise your entire body. The sliding seat works your leg muscles, and the rowing action works the muscles in your arms, shoulders, and back. It's excellent for aerobic fitness and for building muscular strength and endurance. Rowing is also a very good way to burn calories and increase flexibility. However, since rowing involves a fair degree of back flexion, those with recurrent back problems should first check with their physician.

## WEIGHT LIFTING AND FAINTING

**Q** *While working out with weights, I suddenly felt weak and started sweating from head to toe. I feared a "silent heart attack," but my doctor checked me on a treadmill and said I was OK. What happened? I'd like to avoid a repeat.*

**A** You probably performed a so-called Valsalva maneuver when you were lifting weights: If you strain without exhaling, your blood pressure rises and your pulse drops. When you relax—as the weights are lowered—blood pressure can plunge and you're apt to feel faint. Proper breathing while you're lifting weights is essential. Before lifting, take a deep breath and then slowly exhale as you lift. The same warning applies to the use of weight machines.

---

## ✚ *Office* **Visit**

---

# TOO SWEATY
# FOR COMFORT

A 32-YEAR-OLD SECRETARY RECENTLY consulted me for a problem that doesn't sound particularly serious: sweating. But her sweating far, far exceeds the usual physiological response to hot weather, exercise, or anxiety. She sweats constantly, from head to toe, and so profusely that her clothing and hair are almost always dripping wet. Ordinary antiperspirants are useless to stop the flood. Her problem began in her teens. At first, she was able to control it by wearing light, loose-fitting clothes, avoiding exercise, and seeking air-conditioned environments. But gradually those measures stopped working. Understandably, she is now at wit's end. She feels socially isolated, and her boss recently warned that her job is in jeopardy because she must return to her nearby apartment to shower and change her drenched clothes three or four times a day.

My unlucky patient is the victim of what's normally an indispensable method of regulating body temperature. We warm-blooded mammals must operate within a relatively narrow temperature range. If our internal temperature rises much above about 107° F, we die or suffer severe neurological damage. Sweating—which cools us off by evaporation—is one of the body's most effective defenses against overheating.

There are actually two kinds of sweat. One is the slightly salty, watery liquid produced by 2 million eccrine glands found in skin all over the body, especially the palms, soles, face, and armpits. The other is oilier (and smellier) and is produced by the apocrine glands located in the armpits and genital area.

## TOO MUCH OF A GOOD THING

Endocrine disorders, such as an overactive thyroid or a low-blood-sugar reaction to a diabetes medicine, can rev up metabolism to the point where it triggers excess sweating. Sweating can also be a symptom of certain cancers and lymphomas. Chronic infections such as tuberculosis or heart-valve infections are frequently accompanied by sweats.

There are also some oddball causes of excessive sweating, such as eating hot or spicy food or smelling strong perfumes. One long-time patient of mine, now in her 70s, has had paradoxical cold-induced sweating all her life. Her favorite season is high summer, when she can dry out (as long as she stays away from air conditioning). Such rare cases are probably hereditary; her mother had the same problem.

## DRYING OUT

Some types of abnormal sweating are easy to banish. If your face beads up after eating Szechuan food, for example, consider Cantonese cuisine instead. The more perplexing problems arise in people like my 32 year old patient, who is otherwise perfectly healthy. Existing remedies don't always work; even if they do, they have uncomfortable side effects.

The first and mildest option is a prescription antiperspirant called *Drysol*. It contains a 20 percent solution of an aluminum compound—the antiperspirant in over-the-counter products, but at a much higher concentration. *Drysol* works pretty well in mild to moderate cases but gives some users an itchy rash. Another topical method is a procedure called iontophoresis, which uses a mild electrical current to push sweat-gland-paralyzing chemicals into the skin. Iontophoresis is mildly uncomfortable and has to be repeated periodically.

Some prescription ulcer drugs decrease sweat-gland secretion by the same mechanism that they use to dampen the production of stomach acid. These include propantheline *(Probanthine)* and glycopyrrolate *(Robinul)*. But the drugs also cause dry mouth and blurry vision, and can make urination difficult.

## WHEN ALL ELSE FAILS

The ultimate weapons are two much more invasive treatments. One involves the injection of botulinum toxin under the skin, where it blocks the release of a chemical neurotransmitter, acetylcholine, that stimulates sweat glands. (Yes, it's the same substance that causes food poisoning.) One treatment can last up to a year and side effects are minimal. The final step is sympathectomy, surgically severing the spinal nerves that stimulate the problem glands. Afterwards those glands don't produce any sweat, but the affected limbs can get uncomfortably warm while the nonaffected areas may sweat even more.

Because of some recent encouraging reports on botulinum toxin, my patient and I have decided to start with injections into her underarms and groin, the two areas that bother her the most. If that doesn't suffice, she may have to face the prospect of having a sympathectomy.

## Hair care

### IS DYEING DEADLY?

**Q** *Will using hair dye increase my risk of cancer?*

**A** It's possible, but any risk is minuscule and probably confined to one concentrated, permanent color. While chemicals in hair dye can cause cancer in lab animals, studies in humans have not found any risk from popular colors such as brown or blond. One large study several years ago did find that women who used permanent black dye—the most concentrated type—for 20 years or more faced a three-fold increase in the risk of two cancers. However, those malignancies are so rare that the absolute risk rose by less than one in 2 million.

### HAIR-TRANSPLANT SAFETY

**Q** *I'm considering hair-transplant surgery. What are the risks? How can I find a good surgeon?*

**A** Such surgery is safer than it was just a few years ago, partly due to improved grafting techniques. In the most common procedure, the surgeon removes a strip of hair and underlying skin from one part of the scalp, divides that strip into groups of one to four hairs, and implants the groupings into the bald spot. The surgeon then sews or staples together the edges of the donor site; hair usually covers the scar that forms there. There is a very slight risk of infection, numbness, and excessive bleeding. The procedure typically takes two to three sessions, at $4,000 to

$12,000 per session, and is generally not covered by insurance. It may have to be repeated in several years if hair loss continues around the treated region. If you want the operation, choose a surgeon certified by the International Society of Hair Restoration or one who does at least 50 transplants a year. Ask to see live examples (not photos) of the doctor's work, if possible.

## HAIR TODAY, GONE TOMORROW

**Q** *Is there a safe way to remove unwanted hair permanently?*

**A** Electrolysis is the only technique for permanent hair removal. A fine needle inserted into the hair follicle delivers an electrical impulse that kills the hair root.

Even the most skillful electrologist can have problems with the technique. Applying too much electrical stimulation can scar the tissue around the hair follicle. Too little can fail to destroy the root. Rather than risk scarring, it's better to err on the side of understimulation and repeat the procedure if necessary. However, doing so can become a prolonged, expensive process.

## VITAMIN A AND HAIR LOSS

**Q** *I'm a 42-year-old man with thinning hair. I've read that too much vitamin A can cause hair loss. Since I eat large amounts of vegetables that are high in vitamin A, could that be partly responsible for my problem?*

**A** That's highly unlikely. While you could eventually suffer hair loss and other ill effects from taking supplemental megadoses of vitamin A, it's virtually impossible to overdose on the vitamin through the foods you eat. That's because the vitamin A in foods is mostly in the form of certain carotenoids—nontoxic vitamin-A precursors such as beta-carotene. Consuming large amounts of carotenoids can tint your skin orange. But that's not at all harmful, and it's reversible.

Thinning hair in a man your age is most likely due to male-pattern baldness, an inherited trait. Your physician can rule out other, uncommon causes of hair loss, such as an infection.

## Headaches

### FLUORESCENT LIGHTS AND HEADACHES

**Q** *I feel that the fluorescent lights at work give me headaches. Is there any evidence to support that?*

**A** Possibly. The suspected problem is that fluorescent light flickers, although a normally functioning bulb flickers so rapidly that it's not perceived by the human eye. Preliminary evidence is mixed on whether fluorescent lights are more likely to cause headache or other discomfort than other types of lighting. However, any kind of light that's either excessively bright, glaring, or dim may strain the eyes and trigger a headache. To minimize that strain, position your work station to reduce glare from windows or overhead light sources. Or use desk lamps, which can be positioned and adjusted to minimize glare and optimize brightness.

## PREVENTING HANGOVERS

**Q** *What causes hangovers, and can anything help ease or prevent them?*

**A** Alcohol can cause dehydration and disrupt cell function throughout the body, making you feel sick, or hungover, when any intoxication wears off. The amount needed to trigger a hangover depends partly on how much you're used to drinking: As little as one or two glasses of wine, for example, can leave some people feeling wiped out if they seldom drink at all. Of course, the best way to avoid a hangover—and to avoid getting dangerously tipsy—is simply not to drink heavily or more than usual. But several steps may possibly reduce the likelihood and severity of a hangover. Try not to drink on an empty stomach or when you're worn out from exercise or lack of sleep. After you've indulged, drinking lots of nonalcoholic liquids and popping a nonsteroidal anti-inflammatory drug such as aspirin or ibuprofen *(Advil, Motrin IB)* may be helpful. Note that dark liquors including red wine are more likely to leave you hungover than lighter libations.

---

## NOT TONIGHT—I'LL GET A HEADACHE

**Q** *I sometimes get a headache during sexual activity. Your report on special imaging tests mentioned that as one reason to see a doctor. Why?*

**A** To rule out the unlikely possibility of a brain tumor or aneurysm, which can cause headaches during certain types of exertion, such as coughing, bending over, straining during a bowel movement, or having sex. More likely, though, your headaches reflect muscle tension or vascular changes that occur as orgasm nears. "Benign sex headache," as it's called, most often strikes when the victim is tired, under stress, or having repeated intercourse. Some people first notice a dull ache at the back of the head.

If your headaches follow that pattern and a CT or MRI scan shows nothing wrong, you may be able to avoid trouble by taking a breather when you suspect an impending attack or by skipping sex during susceptible times. The prescription drug propranolol *(Inderal)* can usually prevent sex headaches, but it can also diminish potency or impair orgasm. Some people are helped by migraine medications.

## ICE-CREAM HEADACHE

**Q** *What causes the brief but excruciating headache you get when you eat ice cream too fast?*

**A** Sudden, intense facial pain can follow the application of any ice-cold substance to the back of the mouth and the upper part of the throat. Apparently, cold triggers a reflex spasm of the blood vessels there. The pain may result from interrupted blood flow to the tissues. Similar pain can occur in subzero temperatures.

## Health fears and risks

### RISKS AND BENEFITS OF GIVING BLOOD

**Q** *Are there any health benefits or risks to donating blood?*

**A** There are probably no benefits, except for the satisfaction of helping others, and the risks are minor. While some research suggests that giving blood might possibly help prevent cancer and heart disease by lowering the body's iron stores, that possibility is tenuous at best. And donating is generally safe, though it occasionally causes nausea, dizziness, or fainting. To minimize those risks, drink lots of fluids and avoid strenuous activity for several hours after donating.

---

### NIGHT SWEATS

**Q** *I'm a 78-year-old man who experiences recurring night sweats. My doctor can't figure out why. What are the possible causes?*

**A** Several things besides the temperature of your bedroom can spark night sweats. Make sure your doctor has ruled out the most common causes: chronic infections such as tuberculosis, an infected heart valve, or AIDS; and tumors such as lymphomas and kidney or liver cancer. But not all causes are that serious. Using alcohol, aspirin, acetaminophen, or ibuprofen before bedtime can trigger sweating. (In women, night sweats are a common symptom of menopause.)

---

## WHEN TETANUS THREATENS

**Q** *What sort of wounds would require me to get a tetanus shot?*

**A** Puncture wounds caused by nails, large splinters, animal bites, or anything else contaminated with rust, dirt, or animal waste or saliva are the most likely to become infected with tetanus bacteria. Infection can cause stiffness and spasms in the jaw, neck, and other muscles, difficulty breathing, and death. Fortunately, the odds of infection are minuscule if you've maintained your immunity with the recommended series of tetanus vaccinations: three inoculations before age 6, another about six years later, and booster shots every 10 years after that. However, since tetanus is very hard to treat, especially deep or dirty wounds may warrant a booster shot for extra protection if you haven't had one in the past five years. Note that the recent tetanus-vaccine shortage has ended, so if you're due for a booster, call your doctor.

## SMOKING-CESSATION SAFETY

**Q** *I'm a heavy-smoking, overweight man who has had a hemorrhaged cerebral aneurysm [a rupture in an overstretched blood vessel in the brain]. To help me quit smoking, my doctor recommended a nicotine patch (NicoDerm CQ) plus bupropion (Zyban) pills. Is that combination safe?*

**A** Possibly not. Wearing the patch helps wean you from cigarettes by providing a controlled dose of nicotine; bupropion reduces your craving for nicotine and the severity of any withdrawal symptoms. But the combination can cause blood pressure to rise, which potentially could cause a stroke. The two together are generally reserved for people who have a severe addiction to nicotine and haven't been able to quit with the help of either drug alone. Ask your doctor about starting with bupropion, and have your blood pressure checked frequently.

## ASPARTAME SAFETY

**Q** *I use aspartame* (Equal, NutraSweet) *instead of sugar. Is it safe?*

**A** Yes. Aspartame is one of the most thoroughly tested food additives ever approved by the Food and Drug Administration (FDA). Dozens of studies have found it to be safe for the general population. There's no scientific support for the welter of claims, circulating on the Internet, that aspartame can cause everything from headaches and fatigue to birth defects, Alzheimer's disease, and cancer. The only disorder that aspartame can aggravate is phenylketonuria, a rare inherited disorder that can damage the brain. People who have that condition must avoid the amino acid phenylalanine, found in aspartame and many foods.

## GERMS IN PUBLIC PLACES

**Q** *Do germs on commonly used surfaces—like telephone receivers, ATM keypads, and bathroom door handles—pose a threat of infection?*

**A** Yes, but the threat is extremely small. The relatively few bacteria and viruses harmful to humans can survive on dry surfaces for a while—typically several hours or days, but in a few cases for months or even years. Fortunately, the germs cannot multiply without nutrients or moisture. So even if they do manage to enter the body—through the eyes, nose, mouth, genitals, anus, or open wounds—there are usually so few of them that the immune system can wipe them out before any infection develops. To minimize this already minimal risk, wash your hands with soap and water; don't touch your mouth, eyes, or nose with dirty hands; and avoid obviously soiled or moist surfaces, where germs can multiply.

## ALARM OVER SMOKE DETECTORS

*The smoke detectors in my house have small print indicating they contain radioactive material. Is there any concern?*

No. Ionization detectors use a tiny amount of americium 241, a radioactive element, to make the air in a small chamber conduct an electric current. Smoke particles entering the chamber disrupt the current, setting off the alarm. The risk from the minute amount of radiation emitted is negligible. Such exposure is roughly equivalent to moving from one apartment to another one on the floor above, and hence that much closer to the sun.

A far greater risk is relying on ionization smoke detectors alone to protect your family. Ionization devices respond quickly to open flames. But a slow, smoldering fire, the more common type of home fire, is better detected by photoelectric units, which rely on a beam of light and a light-sensitive photocell. Moreover, photoelectric detectors are almost as good as ionization detectors in responding to "fast" fires. When CONSUMER REPORTS last tested smoke detectors, the best performers were either ionization units or combination units with both a photoelectric and an ionization sensor.

## BLOOD SUGAR: HOW LOW IS LOW?

**Q** *In your July report on diabetes, you mention low blood sugar, but don't give an actual number for that condition. What's the threshold?*

**A** Low blood sugar is technically defined as any value below 60 milligrams per deciliter of blood. But low blood sugar doesn't require treatment unless it's actually causing symptoms—sweating, palpitations, and hunger—which appear at variable levels below 60 mg. in different individuals. People with symptomatic low blood sugar should be evaluated by an endocrinologist to determine the underlying cause.

## FEAR OF FIBERGLASS

**Q** *The fiberglass insulation in my basement ceiling is exposed. Because my wife's throat sometimes feels scratchy when she works in the basement, she won't let the children play there for fear the fiberglass is harmful. Is it?*

**A** Probably not in this situation. Studies have shown a possible link between exposure to fiberglass and lung cancer, but only in workers who inhale huge amounts of the fibers for many years during manufacture or installation. Fiberglass insulation that is fixed in place usually doesn't give off airborne particles.

## NORMAL BODY TEMPERATURE

**Q** *My temperature never seems to reach the "normal" level of 98.6° F. In fact, I rarely get a reading much higher than 97.5° or so, unless I'm sick. Is this unusual?*

**A** Not at all. The time-honored "normal" oral temperature of 98.6° F represented the average for healthy people, and that number has been revised downward to 98.2°. Some perfectly healthy people never break 98.0°. In addition, your normal body temperature can vary, depending in part on the time of day: It's consistently lowest in the morning and highest in the late afternoon or evening. That daily variation can range anywhere from about 0.7° to 2.6° F.

---

## ✚ *Office* **Visit**

# LYME DISEASE: BEYOND THE RASH

SYPHILIS HAS BEEN CALLED the "great imitator" because its varied symptoms can masquerade as many other diseases, but Lyme disease may be a contender to take over that title. Consider these two recent cases:

Last summer a 26-year-old graduate student collapsed in a local bookstore. In the ambulance on the way to the emergency room, he needed life-saving cardiopulmonary resuscitation. An electrocardiogram showed the upper chambers of his heart were beating independently of his lower chambers, slowing his heart to the point where it was barely able to sustain life, let alone consciousness. The immediate insertion of a temporary pacemaker returned his heartbeat to normal. He had hiked in the woods two weeks before but didn't recall a tick bite.

Later that month I saw a 56-year-old dentist with left-sided acute sciatica, pain that began in his left buttock and radiated down his leg to just below his knee. Imaging tests of his lower spine were normal, yet he did have abnormal reflexes in that leg. Blood workup was negative, including a test for Lyme disease. Finally, I sent him to a neurologist, who, wisely, performed a spinal tap that was positive for Lyme disease.

## LYME: A COMMON DISEASE

Lyme disease is endemic in the Northeast and North Central parts of the country, where the ticks that harbor the infecting bacterium, Borrelia burgdorferi, abound. With over 23,000 cases reported in 2002, Lyme is the most commonly reported insect-borne infection in the U.S.

The disease has two distinct phases, acute and chronic, both of which have highly variable symptoms. The best-known early symptom, the bull's-eye rash, affects about 80 percent of victims. Other early symptoms can include all, some, or none of the following: headache, chills and fever, acute arthritis, and sore muscles. If not recognized or treated promptly, Lyme can lead to neurological and cardiac complications.

## HEART AND NERVE SYMPTOMS

The most common nerve complication is paralysis of the facial nerve, or Bell's palsy. The bacterium can also attack nerve roots adjacent to the spine, causing the kind of pain that afflicted our dentist; and peripheral nerves in the hands and feet, causing numbness and tingling.

Lyme affects the heart in an estimated 10 percent of infected people, usually by impairing the impulse-conduction system. Symptoms can range from undetectable to severe. Less often Lyme disease can affect the heart muscle itself or cause inflammation of the pericardium, or heart lining. Disturbances in heart rhythm can occur, but rarely so severely as to cause life-threatening symptoms as it did in our graduate student.

## LYME DISEASE OF THE BRAIN?

Controversy has existed for years about the existence of so-called chronic Lyme disease encephalopathy, or brain inflammation, that persists long after antibiotic treatment has eradicated all trace of the bacterium. People who believe they have this condition complain of such vague symptoms as the inability to concentrate, fatigue, memory loss, and sleep problems. Experts have yet to arrive at a definition of this syndrome, much less diagnostic criteria. One thing is known: Repeated courses of intravenous antibiotics in such cases, though plied by some aggressive self-styled Lyme disease experts, are useless, expensive, and nonreimbursable.

## SYMPTOMS OF CONCERN

If you live in a part of the U.S. that has had recognized cases of Lyme, be sure your doctor bears that in mind if you have:

- A rash resembling a bull's-eye—that expands over a few days.
- Flu-like symptoms not in flu season.
- Acute arthritis.
- Acute onset of sciatica or any other inflammation involving a single nerve or groups of nerves.
- Bell's palsy.
- An abnormal electrocardiogram indicating problems with the conduction system or abnormal heart rhythm.

The graduate student was treated with one month of daily intravenous injections of ceftriaxone, a potent antibiotic. His heart block disappeared in one week and the temporary pacemaker was withdrawn after a month. During a month's treatment with oral tetracycline, the dentist's pain gradually abated. He was back to work in three weeks and has had no recurrences to date.

---

## ✚ *Office* **Visit**

---

# THE NIGHT
# THE CAT DIED

ONE WINTER NIGHT SEVERAL YEARS AGO, I was awakened at 3 a.m.
by a call from the emergency room about two patients, a middle-
aged dentist and his wife. They had eaten dinner that night at a
local restaurant, returned to their apartment at about 11 p.m., fed
the cat, and went to bed. An hour or so later, they both awoke
with nausea and headache severe enough to prompt the ER visit.
Since they had eaten identical meals, the ER physician suspected a
food-borne infection. After treatment with antinausea medication
and intravenous fluids, the couple felt better and were sent home.
I complimented the ER doctor on a job well done and hung up,
thankful there was no need for me to venture forth into the cold.

Shortly after drifting back to sleep, I was again jolted awake by
a ringing phone. This time it was the dentist himself. He and his
wife were again feeling ill. Indeed, the wife was not only
headachy and nauseated but was crying hysterically because, on
their arrival home from the ER, they had found their cat dead. A
light clicked on in my brain. I told them to open all the windows
and phone 911 immediately. By the time I met them at the ER, it
was clear my suspicion of carbon monoxide poisoning was correct. Had they remained at home, they would have died.

## A COMMON POISON

Carbon monoxide is one of the most common causes of poisoning in the U.S. Every year more than 5,000 people die from carbon monoxide inhalation (only about 10 percent of these fatali-

ties are accidental). The number of near misses, like my patients', is unknown but may be as many as 10,000 per year.

Invisible, odorless, and nonirritating, carbon monoxide is a uniquely insidious poison. Inhaled, it's readily absorbed into the bloodstream. Once there, it displaces oxygen from hemoglobin, the protein that transports oxygen throughout the body. In the absence of oxygen, our tissues, including brain, heart, and muscle, soon suffocate and cease to function.

Carbon monoxide results from the incomplete burning of carbon-based fuel such as gasoline, wood, or paper. Normally, blood levels of carbon monoxide rarely exceed 1 to 3 percent. Pack-a-day cigarette smokers commonly have levels of 10 to 12 percent. The dentist and his wife had blood levels of 17 percent—enough to cause headache, nausea, and vomiting. Above 20 to 25 percent concentration, cognition and memory become impaired. Above those levels, cardiac and neurological problems abound, followed by coma and death.

## FINDING THE SOURCE

Any area that contains a car, barbecue, lawn mower, gas stove, hot water heater, furnace, fireplace, or snow blower is capable of emitting deadly carbon monoxide fumes not only into the immediate surroundings, such as a garage or basement, but also any attached living quarters. (However, a recent case of carbon monoxide poisoning in two children resulted from exposure to jet-ski exhaust, an accident that should spur everyone to avoid inhaling motor fumes even in the great outdoors.)

In my patients' case, as we learned the next day, firefighters found increased air levels of carbon monoxide in the apartment, though no apparent source was evident. Receiving no response from the adjacent apartment, they broke in. The kitchen stove, which shared a common vent with our patients' apartment, was on. The occupant, an elderly woman, was dead.

## TREATMENT AND PREVENTION

Treatment of acute carbon monoxide poisoning consists of re-oxygenating the blood as quickly as possible. Because carbon monoxide sticks to hemoglobin much more tenaciously than oxygen itself, once levels exceed about 20 percent, treatment with high-pressure (hyperbaric) oxygen is required. In my patients' case, high-flow 100 percent oxygen did the trick. They were released from the hospital the next day and have had no permanent ill effects.

To prevent problems, never use a gas or charcoal grill in an enclosed space, and be sure to regularly have your furnace serviced. Don't idle your car or lawn mower in an attached garage, even with the door open.

You should also have at least one carbon monoxide monitor in your home. CONSUMER REPORTS last reviewed those $30 to $50 devices in October 2001 and found all major brands worked adequately. If the alarm ever goes off, throw open all the windows and doors at once and get everyone out of the house. Then summon your local fire department.

## Heartburn

### ETERNAL HEARTBURN THERAPY?

**Q** *I've been taking the prescription acid-reducer omeprazole (Prilosec) for about a year. It works great, but will I ever be able to stop taking it without suffering?*

**A** Probably, but it depends on the underlying condition you're being treated for. If it is chronic heartburn, you may need to take the drug indefinitely—or for one- to two-month periods when your symptoms flare up. With ulcers, the drug can usually lower the acidity of your stomach and upper gastrointestinal tract enough to allow any sores, scars, or irritations to heal. Then you can stop taking it, or switch to a less potent drug. In either case talk to your doctor about gradually stepping down from your current regimen, perhaps by taking half a dose, then alternating every other day with ranitidine *(Zantac)* or another mild acid-reducer.

### SURGERY FOR HEARTBURN

**Q** *Should I consider surgery for my severe, chronic heartburn?*

**A** Only if all else fails: when lifestyle changes and drugs either don't provide relief or cause intolerable side effects. Surgery tightens the muscles that keep acid from entering the esophagus. But lifestyle changes plus drugs can reduce stomach acid enough to banish the burn, at least in the short run, just as effectively as surgery. Moreover, the longest and best study of such surgery found that only one-third of patients remained heartburn-free a decade later; the rest still needed to take drugs regularly to control their symptoms. And surgery is no more likely than drugs to prevent damage to the esophagus, which increases the risk of cancer.

Lifestyle steps include avoiding large meals and aggravating foods, not lying down right after eating, elevating the head of your bed, and stopping smoking. Heartburn drugs include antacids containing calcium carbonate, magnesium, or aluminum hydroxide, alone or in combination *(Maalox, Mylanta, Tums);* H2-blockers, such as nizatidine *(Axid)* and ranitidine *(Zantac);* and proton-pump inhibitors, such as lansoprazole *(Prevacid)* and omeprazole *(Prilosec).*

## HEARTBURN DRUGS AND LOST NUTRIENTS

**Q** *My mother takes lansoprazole* (Prevacid), *which eases chronic heartburn by reducing secretion of stomach acid. But I've heard that reduced stomach acid can contribute to nutritional deficiencies in older people. Should we be worried?*

**A** Probably not. Long-term studies have generally not shown any significant nutritional deficiencies in patients taking acid-reducing medications at any age, with the possible exception of vitamin B12. It's also known that aging itself can result in low vitamin B12 blood levels. This is due to loss of the cells that produce a factor that facilitates B12 absorption further down the intestine.

# Liver disorders

## GILBERT'S SYNDROME

**Q** *I was recently diagnosed with Gilbert's syndrome. My doctor says it's harmless. Is that true?*

**A** Yes—and it may actually provide some health benefits. Gilbert's syndrome increases the blood level of bilirubin, a yellow pigment in bile, by harmlessly reducing the liver's ability to dispose of the pigment. A potent antioxidant, bilirubin may help prevent cell damage and clogging of the arteries. Preliminary studies indicate that people with Gilbert's may have up to an 80 percent reduction in heart-disease risk. Other studies have linked high bilirubin levels with lower rates of cancer and heart attack, though only in men for unknown reasons.

## TEST FOR LIVER DISEASE

**Q** *For several years, blood tests have shown that I have a slightly elevated level of the liver enzyme known as SGPT. But all of the other tests for liver disease have found nothing wrong with me. My doctor says it's not uncommon for a healthy person to have an elevated SGPT count. Is he right?*

**A** Most likely. In obese people it may be due to accumulation of fat in the liver. If you've tested negative for hepatitis A, B, and C, you have nothing to worry about. However, to be sure, your liver function should be retested periodically.

## Medical procedures

### ROTATOR-CUFF SURGERY

**Q** *I'm a 69-year-old man with a torn rotator cuff in my shoulder, which keeps me from doing many of the activities I enjoy. After treatment with rofecoxib (Vioxx) failed to ease the pain, my orthopedist recommended surgery to repair the tear. Would that be a good choice at my age?*

**A** Quite possibly, particularly if the pain precludes physical therapy, the usual option before surgery. Physical therapy can often strengthen the remaining muscle fibers sufficiently to restore function; complete tears almost always require surgery. Some 10 percent develop postsurgical complications, such as increased shoulder pain and stiffness or nerve damage that can cause pain in the neck, arm, or hand. These risks are slightly higher in older people, who also tend to heal more slowly and to require more postoperative physical therapy. However, the operation succeeds in reducing pain and restoring function about 90 percent of the time overall, and only slightly less often in older patients. So for the average person of your age, the odds are very favorable.

### LESS PAINFUL BLOOD DRAW

**Q** *My veins, which look adequate, are difficult to draw blood from since they tend to roll. Is there anything I can do to make it easier and less painful?*

**A** Unfortunately, you're stuck with your troublesome veins, so there's little that can be done. An experienced, certified phlebotomist should know how to "anchor" rolling veins, so if you have blood drawn often, try to find one who can do it successfully every time. If you don't have a reliable phlebotomist, ask for an experienced technician and warn that person that your blood is "hard to get." Keeping your arm warm before the technician draws your blood may also help.

## LESS-PAINFUL BIOPSY

**Q** *I find biopsies of the prostate gland extremely painful. Your recent report on prostate cancer suggested using the topical anesthetic lidocaine to reduce the pain, but my urologist cannot figure out how that would be done. Please clarify.*

**A** Your urologist can apply lidocaine gel directly onto the rectal wall during a digital examination about 10 minutes before the procedure. That way the numbing effect can reduce the discomfort of both the entry of the probe and the cutting action of the biopsy itself. A recent study found that this approach significantly reduced the pain. (Note that many men do not find prostate biopsy extremely painful; the discomfort is often likened to that caused by a rubber band snapped against the skin; in addition, the biopsy site may ache after the procedure.)

## STRESS-TEST SAFETY

**Q** *I'm a healthy 74-year-old man who works out twice a week. During the exercise my heart doesn't race and I have no trouble breathing, yet my doctor wants me to undergo an exercise-stress test. Do the possible benefits of the test justify the risk that it might trigger a heart attack?*

**A** Exercise stress tests—in which an electrocardiogram (EKG) is taken during strenuous exertion, usually on a treadmill—can detect heart abnormalities that could make exercise dangerous unless you took special precautions. But like any physically demanding activity, the test does pose a very slight risk of heart attack. Further, it identifies only a minority of endangered people. And it sometimes finds apparent abnormalities that turn out, on further testing, to pose no real danger at all. So the test is generally worthwhile only for people who have experienced chest pain (especially during exercise), are sedentary and want to start exercising vigorously, or have either coronary heart disease or more than one risk factor for the disease (see page 143 for those risk factors).

## NONINVASIVE ANGIOGRAPHY

**Q** *Your recent article on tests for heart disease discussed electron-beam computed tomography (EBCT) but didn't mention noninvasive angiography. Why not?*

**A** The two terms refer to the same procedure. Standard angiography, or cardiac catheterization, typically ordered after an exercise stress test reveals a potential coronary problem, is mildly invasive. Using a catheter snaked up into the coronary arteries, cardiologists inject dye to outline those vessels on an X-ray or computed tomography (CT) scan. That enables doctors to inspect the arteries for blockages.

No dye is used in noninvasive angiography, or EBCT. Instead, a special CT scan measures the calcium buildup in the artery walls. Calcium is a major component of plaque deposits in the arteries, and levels of the mineral there correlate fairly well with the extent of the blockage. But EBCT doesn't provide the detailed coronary information that the stress test plus standard angiography does. And no one knows whether basing treatment decisions on calcium measurements alone is effective or wise. Our consultants say that EBCT may help indicate when to intensify treatment in patients at moderate risk of heart attack. But it shouldn't substitute for the proven combination of the other two tests.

---

**✚** *Office* **Visit**

# WHO NEEDS A STRESS TEST?

AFTER UNDERGOING A PHYSICAL examination, a 52-year-old stockbroker announced to me that he was ready to join a gym and give up his lifelong sedentary existence. One hitch: The gym required my approval. He felt fine, and the examination had not disclosed any startling abnormalities; his cholesterol, blood pressure, and electrocardiogram were all normal.

But because his father had died in his 50s of a heart attack, I told him that a stress test was in order. We were both surprised when the test turned out to be markedly positive, indicating serious coronary disease. An angiogram showed a partial blockage of his left main coronary artery—the vessel that supplies blood to virtually all of the heart muscle. A close call: He doubtless would have died in the gym during his first minutes of exercise.

Stress tests date from the early 1930s, when Dr. Arthur Masters devised a standardized method of hitching patients to an electro-cardiograph while they climbed on and off a two-step wooden platform. It wasn't until the 1960s that the platform was replaced by a self-propelled treadmill, which was later replaced by the motorized version.

More-recent embellishments include echocardiography with exercise to show the valves and muscular wall of the heart and the injection of nuclear material at peak exercise to study the distribution of the radioactivity (or lack of it) in the scanned areas of the heart muscle. But the underlying goal remains the same: to put the heart under controlled stress and see if anything happens that suggests an inadequate blood supply to the heart.

## WHO GETS THE TEST?

A lot of people undergo stress testing every year. In 1998 more than 530,000 treadmill exercise tests were performed just on Medicare recipients.

It would be nice to report that the individuals who got the expensive stress echocardiogram ($900) or nuclear stress test ($1,600) were exactly the ones who needed them, but the facts suggest otherwise. In one survey, stress-test rates depended more on the doctor's specialty than on medical need: Cardiologists were nearly eight times more likely to order those tests than were internists.

Whites are more likely than minorities to get the tests, and men more likely than women. People with plenty of insurance get tested more than those with no insurance at all. People who live in locations that have facilities for angiography and bypass surgery get the tests more often than people who don't.

## PRIME CANDIDATES

Aside from its use in patients who have known coronary disease or who have had angioplasty or bypass surgery, the stress test is most useful for evaluating chest pain in people with no history of heart disease. Yet in one survey only one-quarter of outpatient cardiac stress testing was for that indication. For patients with chest pain that's typical for coronary artery disease—a dull, pressurelike pain or discomfort in the center of the chest that radiates to the left arm, neck, or jaw, increases with exertion, and disappears with rest—a stress test may not be necessary and might even be dangerous. Such patients should probably proceed directly to an angiogram.

The stress test comes in handiest with so-called atypical chest pain—pain that doesn't fit the typical profile—particularly in women. And when such pain occurs in someone with multiple coronary risk factors—such as a family history of heart attack at age 60 or less, diabetes, smoking, high LDL cholesterol, hypertension, low HDL cholesterol, and possibly obesity and high triglycerides—the likelihood of a positive (worrisome) test increases markedly. In a person who has vague chest pains and no risk factors, the likelihood that a stress test will indicate coronary disease is low and the test may not even be worth doing.

Stress testing is also appropriate for some patients who have no chest pain at all. Those include people facing surgery who have coronary risk factors, and older people with public-safety jobs, such as airline pilots or bus drivers. The "worried well" may require the reassurance that only a negative stress test can provide. Finally, sedentary people who decide to take up aerobic exercise in middle age, such as our stockbroker, should probably get the test before they start working out.

After bypass surgery, he finally made it to the gym, as part of a rehabilitative program; he was relieved that his original decision to exercise had uncovered a potentially lethal blockage.

## Medications and immunizations

### PAIN RELIEVERS AND REYE'S SYNDROME

*Q* *Is there any evidence that over-the-counter pain relievers other than aspirin may contribute to the risk of developing Reye's syndrome in children?*

*A* No. Aspirin is the only analgesic shown to increase the risk of Reye's, a potentially fatal disease. But youngsters up to age 18 need to avoid aspirin only when they have a fever or a viral illness; the drug does not appear to cause Reye's syndrome at other times. Note that aspirin is a common ingredient in many cold and flu remedies. So youngsters' parents and adolescents themselves should check the labels for aspirin as well as its other names: acetylsalicylate, acetylsalicylic acid, salicylic acid, and salicylate.

### PILLS FOR OSTEOPENIA?

*Q* *I've been taking estrogen-replacement therapy for 10 years. A year ago I started taking risedronate (Actonel) to treat osteopenia. My latest test showed no change in the bone density. Should I continue taking the risedronate, since it's not improving the problem?*

*A* Possibly. Osteopenia, or mild bone thinning, requires treatment if it's getting worse. While risedronate potentially can increase bone density, simply stopping further loss could be considered an "improvement." It's hard to tell whether the stabilization stems from the risedronate or the estrogen, which also fights bone loss. However, taking estrogen increases the risk of developing breast cancer. And risedronate appears to fight bone loss better than estrogen does. So if you don't need estrogen to ease menopausal symptoms, talk to your doctor about stopping the hormone and continuing on risedronate. After your next bone-density measurement in a year or two, your doctor can decide whether you still need that drug.

## LIVER-DAMAGING DRUGS

Q  *In your recent article on the liver, you listed some drugs that can harm it. But you didn't mention the antifungals itraconazole* (Sporanox) *and terbinafine* (Lamisil). *Can't they threaten the liver, too?*

A  Yes, along with many other drugs that are similarly less common than the ones we listed. The two antifungals—used to treat nail, skin, and systemic fungal infections—have recently been linked to several cases of liver failure, many of them fatal. As a result, the FDA now recommends that doctors order lab tests to confirm a fungal infection before prescribing either drug, and additional tests to rule out pre-existing liver disease before prescribing terbinafine tablets. (The cream and spray versions haven't caused such problems.) Patients taking either drug should immediately report any of these symptoms of liver problems to their doctor: persistent nausea, anorexia, fatigue, vomiting, right upper-abdominal pain, jaundice (yellowish complexion), dark urine, or pale stools. In addition, it appears that itraconazole can also damage the heart, so don't take the drug if you have congestive heart failure. Patients who develop any of the following heart-failure symptoms while on itraconazole should similarly consult their doctor: swelling in the feet, ankles, legs, or abdomen; severe indigestion; or extreme shortness of breath, especially when lying down.

## EXPIRED DRUGS

**Q** *I try to buy vitamins and nonprescription drugs for my family in huge containers. But they often sit around for years, reaching their expiration date before we finish them. Would taking expired pills do us any harm?*

**A** Probably not, since they're unlikely to turn toxic. However, they might not supply the expected benefit, because all drugs and vitamins gradually break down and lose strength over time. The expiration date estimates when the potency will dwindle to about 90 or 95 percent of its original strength, under average conditions. Storage under ideal, manufacturer-recommended conditions—usually in a dry, cool place—can extend that date by about a year. Regardless of age, any drug or vitamin that shows signs of spoilage should be tossed out. Such signs include vinegary-smelling aspirin, crumbly tablets, sticky or melted capsules, or anything that has started to change color. Even without such signs, experts recommend discarding any drug or vitamin that's more than two years old.

## ANTIBIOTICS AND "GOOD" BACTERIA

**Q** *I'm taking an antibiotic, which might be wiping out my body's helpful bacteria. Should I consider taking probiotic pills or eating yogurt to help restore the beneficial bugs?*

**A** Possibly, depending on which drug you're taking, your susceptibility to certain side effects, and your willingness to pay the probiotics price—about $13 per week. The most common side effect of antibiotics is diarrhea caused by the loss of beneficial bacteria in the gut, striking anywhere from 5 to 30 percent of patients. The risk is highest with antibiotics such as clindamycin, cephalosporins and penicillins and lowest with aminoglycosides and fluoroquinolones.

Probiotic supplements and fermented dairy products such as many brands of yogurt and kefir all contain live microbes. But only two organisms—the bacterium Lactobacillus GG *(Culturelle)* and the yeast Saccharomyces boulardii *(Florastor)*—have proved hardy enough to survive both the digestive acids and the antibiotic onslaught. (Yogurt sold in Europe contains Lactobacillus GG, but yogurt in the U.S. doesn't.) Both can reduce the incidence of antibiotic-related diarrhea by up to 60 percent.

To increase the odds of the microbes surviving, take the pills midway between successive antibiotic doses. Note that these supplements have caused systemic infection in a few cases. So avoid them if you have a disease that weakens immunity, such as diabetes, HIV, or certain cancers; if you're taking corticosteroids long-term; or if you have damaged or artificial heart valves.

## FOSAMAX FOREVER?

**Q** *I'm a 64-year-old woman taking alendronate for bone loss. Will I ever be able to stop taking it without risking a fracture?*

**A** Not likely. Alendronate *(Fosamax)* and risedronate *(Actonel)* have replaced hormone therapy as the preferred treatment for bone loss. But while those drugs can stop the loss and even help rebuild bone, they don't fix the cause of the breakdown. So once you stop taking them, your bones will continue to weaken. Since both drugs are relatively new, no one knows whether decades of use will cause any ill effects. But studies lasting up to seven years have found no negative consequences from daily use. And once-a-week dosing, which is more convenient, appears to be just as safe and effective.

## WHEN TO USE ANTIBIOTIC SALVES

**Q** *Do I really need to apply antibiotic ointment every time I get a cut, scrape, or burn?*

**A** No, and sometimes it can actually be detrimental. For dirty wounds—those containing visible dirt or grit—applying antibiotic ointment is a good idea, since it sharply reduces the risk of infection, which occurs in about 20 to 30 percent of those wounds. But in clean wounds, the risk is only about 1 to 5 percent, so the drawbacks of the ointments can outweigh the benefits. In particular, allergic reactions occur in roughly 4 to 6 percent of people who use the antibiotic neomycin, found in *Mycitracin* and *Neosporin*, and 2 percent of those who use the antibiotic bacitracin, found in those ointments as well as some *Betadine* and *Polysporin* brands. Moreover, all antibiotics may contribute to the emergence of antibiotic-resistant strains of harmful bacteria. Whether or not you apply ointment to a minor cut, scrape, or burn, first wash the wound with soap and warm water to eliminate all visible grime and grit. If the injury is deep or extensive, rinse with water only, and seek medical attention right away.

## ADULT IMMUNIZATIONS

**Q** *How often do adults need to have a tetanus shot?*

**A** All adults should receive a tetanus-diphtheria toxoid booster every 10 years. If an injury that might lead to tetanus occurs more than five years after the last shot, another booster should be given. (The next shot would then be given 10 years from that date.)

## SUPPLEMENTAL BLOOD THINNERS

**Q** *Each day I take 325 milligrams (mg) of aspirin, 2 mg of garlic oil, and 120 mg of ginkgo biloba. I take the aspirin as a blood thinner, but since the garlic and ginkgo have a similar effect, could I eliminate the aspirin?*

**A** If your doctor prescribed the aspirin to prevent or treat cardiovascular disease, definitely keep taking it. Aspirin is a potent, proven, and abundantly studied blood thinner or clot inhibitor. The possible anticlotting abilities of garlic and ginkgo have not been carefully studied, so the effects are unpredictable, and there are no dosage recommendations. If anything, abandon the supplements, since taking them together with aspirin may increase your risk of bleeding.

## JUST ONE SHOT FOR PNEUMONIA?

**Q** *You've said that people 65 and older should receive pneumococcal vaccine just once. But some doctors have told me they recommend the shot every five years. I had one six years ago when I was 71. Should I get another?*

**A** Healthy older people generally need only one dose of pneumococcal vaccine. (However, a single revaccination with the "23-valent" vaccine is worth considering if you previously received the older, "14-valent" type of pneumococcal vaccine.) But if you have a medical condition such as heart, kidney, liver, or lung disease, diabetes, Hodgkin's disease, cerebrospinal fluid leaks, an immune-system disorder, or sickle-cell anemia, you could be susceptible to complications from pneumonia. Anyone in those risk groups should get a shot every six years.

## FLU SHOTS

**Q** *I've heard so many opinions, pro and con, about flu shots. Who should get a flu shot? How effective is it? When is the best time to get one?*

**A** Anyone who can tolerate a flu shot should consider getting one before the influenza season begins. That's especially important for these high-risk groups:

• People age 50 or over.

• People with chronic lung or heart disorders, including children with asthma.

• Adults and children who, during the preceding year, needed regular medical care or hospitalization for a chronic disease: diabetes, kidney disorders, sickle-cell disease, or suppressed immune systems (including HIV/AIDS).

• Children and teenagers 6 months to 18 years who are on long-term aspirin therapy.

• People who live with or care for a person at high risk. A flu shot takes about two weeks to provide protection and lasts about six months. But the injection does not provide full immunity in all cases. It's about 90 percent effective in young, healthy people, and 70 percent effective in elderly, high-risk people—for the strains of influenza included in the vaccine. If an unexpected strain of flu pops up during the flu season, the vaccine may not work at all.

Generally, October is the best time for a flu shot, but any time between September and February is better than not at all. Travelers abroad, however, should consider a flu shot whatever the month. They may risk exposure to the virus at any time of year.

## CAN YOU TOLERATE A FLU SHOT?

**Q** *You say that "anyone who can tolerate a flu shot" should consider getting one. Exactly who can't tolerate a flu shot?*

**A** People allergic to eggs, which are used to make the influenza vaccine, should not receive the shot. And people with an acute illness, such as a respiratory, gastrointestinal, or urinary-tract infection, should wait until they recover. Pregnant women should delay a flu shot until after the first trimester, unless they are at high risk.

---

## Men's health

## CALCIUM AND PROSTATE CANCER

**Q** *I read that calcium raises your prostate-cancer risk. Should I consume less of it?*

**A** Probably not. Several studies have linked increased calcium intake, from milk or supplements, with an increased chance of prostate cancer. But similar studies have found no such link, and it's unclear how calcium might promote that cancer. Further, the mineral appears to have the opposite effect on colon cancer. And over 12 percent of men will eventually break a bone weakened by osteoporosis, in part because they don't consume enough calcium: 1,000 milligrams (mg) a day before they reach age 50, 1,200 mg from age 50 to 65, and 1,500 mg after age 65.

Foods that may help ward off prostate cancer include those rich in the phytochemicals lycopene (apricots, pink grapefruit, tomatoes, watermelon), quercetin (beans, citrus fruit, green leafy vegetables), or sulfurophane (broccoli, brussels sprouts, cabbage, cauliflower, kale), or in the mineral selenium (Brazil nuts, lean meats, seafood, sunflower seeds, whole-wheat products).

## DOES SEX SOOTHE THE PROSTATE?

**Q** *My urologist says having sex frequently is good for benign enlargement or inflammation of the prostate gland. Is he right?*

**A** Possibly. Many men with those conditions report that ejaculation temporarily eases symptoms such as difficulty urinating and prostate pain. And one small study found that 14 of 18 sexually inactive men with prostatitis experienced at least moderate symptom relief after six months of ejaculating at least twice a week. One possible reason: Ejaculation stimulates muscles and nerves in the prostate region and eases pressure in the gland by releasing built-up semen. But while having sex or masturbating may possibly soothe symptoms, you should see a urologist to treat the underlying problem. For enlargement, treatment may include the herbal supplement saw palmetto; drugs such as doxazosin *(Cardura)*, finasteride *(Proscar)*, tamsulosin *(Flomax)*, or terazosin *(Hytrin)*; or in severe cases, surgery. A course of antibiotics may cure inflammation.

## PROSTATE PROBLEMS

**Q** *Can urinary or sexual habits affect the incidence or severity of an enlarged prostate or any other prostate problems?*

**A** Those personal habits have nothing to do with the development of any prostate problems. However, modifying certain habits may help reduce the severity of symptoms. For example, urinating more frequently to keep the bladder from overfilling, allowing enough time to empty the bladder completely, and cutting back on fluids for several hours before bedtime can help reduce symptoms from an enlarged prostate. And since congestion in the prostate gland can aggravate the discomfort from chronic prostatitis (inflammation often due to bacterial infection), many urologists recommend frequent ejaculations to minimize that discomfort.

## MICROWAVING THE PROSTATE

**Q** *Is microwave treatment for enlarged prostate safe and effective?*

**A** That's not yet clear. This relatively new procedure is an alternative to traditional prostate surgery, which may help when medication or watchful waiting fails to control urinary symptoms. In the traditional method, an instrument inserted through the penis cuts away excess prostate tissue. The newer technique takes the same route, but uses a microwave-emitting antenna to heat and destroy the excess tissue.

In preliminary studies, surgery reduced symptoms roughly 20 percent more than the microwave method. Microwaving does pose less risk of side effects, such as impotence, incontinence, and retrograde ejaculation (semen traveling backward into the bladder). However, the urinary symptoms are more likely to recur and require further treatment. Until the technique's long-term effectiveness is known, our medical consultants recommend sticking with traditional surgery.

## PROSTATECTOMY AND INFERTILITY

**Q** *You recently said that after surgery for an enlarged prostate, virtually all men become infertile due to "retrograde ejaculation," in which semen travels up into the bladder. Aren't there ways to isolate semen from the urine for artificial insemination?*

**A** Yes. But the reliability of those techniques varies from person to person, depending on the viability of the sperm. Men who want to father a child after prostate surgery may want to consider storing sperm at a sperm bank before the operation. However, that's not a sure bet either, since freezing and thawing make sperm less vigorous.

## HIGH PSA AND PROSTATE CANCER

**Q** *My doctor ordered a PSA blood test for prostate cancer during a routine physical exam last fall. The results showed a score of 28, so he ordered a biopsy; it revealed no sign of cancer. I've since had another PSA test, which came out just as high. What, if anything, should I do about it?*

**A** Talk to your doctor about having another biopsy—soon. A PSA (prostate-specific antigen) score above 10 indicates a strong probability of prostate cancer. The repeat biopsy should be guided by rectal ultrasound, which can help identify any suspicious areas in the prostate.

## VASECTOMY AND PROSTATE CANCER

**Q** *I am considering getting a vasectomy. But according to a release form for the procedure, "Some studies have suggested*

*an increased risk of prostate cancer in men who have undergone
vasectomy." Should I avoid the operation?*

**A** No. There's no plausible reason why vasectomy, which involves cutting and tying the tubes that carry sperm, would
increase prostate-cancer risk. Men who undergo vasectomy tend
to be health-conscious people who see their doctors frequently.
So the higher cancer rate found in some studies probably just reflects better diagnosis of prostate cancer in those men, rather than
any cancer-causing potential of the procedure itself. A recent review by the National Institutes of Health concluded that the overall evidence suggests no association between vasectomy and the
cancer. The 20-minute procedure, typically done in a doctor's office under local anesthesia, remains one of the most effective
means of birth control, with an average reliability of 99 percent.

## IMPOTENCE AND BLOOD-PRESSURE DRUGS

**Q** *The medication I take for high blood pressure is making me
impotent. Is there a drug that can control my blood pressure
without affecting my sex life?*

**A** All of the widely used types of blood-pressure drugs have been
associated in varying degrees with impotence. However, two
classes of antihypertensive drugs may be less likely to cause impotence. One is a group known as ACE inhibitors, such as captopril
*(Capoten)*, enalapril *(Vasotec)*, and lisinopril *(Prinivil, Fosinopril)*.
The other group, called calcium-channel blockers, includes such
drugs as diltiazem *(Cardizem)*, nicardipine *(Cardene)*, nifedipine
*(Procardia)*, and verapamil *(Calan, Isoptin)*. If your current medication can be safely changed to one of those without compromising blood-pressure control, switching may solve your problem. If

not, your physician might consider prescribing one of the impotence drugs, such as sildenafil, better known by its brand name, *Viagra.*

## PEYRONIE'S DISEASE

**Q** *What can you tell me about Peyronie's disease?*

**A** Peyronie's disease is a common disorder in which the penis becomes curved and distorted, especially when erect. The cause is unknown.

Local injections of steroids or calcium-channel blockers are sometimes successful. In carefully selected patients, surgery can sometimes be effective. It shouldn't be ruled out simply because of age. An experienced surgeon is necessary because of the possibility that surgery may create more scar tissue. When Peyronie's disease is combined with erectile dysfunction, the standard treatment is a penile implant. The recovery time for either procedure is about two weeks. Ask your doctor to refer you to a urologist experienced in treating this disease, or check the directory of the American Board of Medical Specialties, available at many libraries, and on the Internet at *www.abms.org* or *www.boardcertifieddocs.com,* for a list of board-certified specialists in your area.

## Neurological problems

### TAMING TREMORS

**Q** *I have essential tremor, which makes it hard for me to write.
Is there any treatment for this condition?*

**A** There's no cure for essential tremor, which may be geneti-
cally caused and can occur at any age. However, daily doses
of the beta-blocker propranolol *(Inderal)* and the anticonvulsive
drug primidone *(Mysoline)*—taken alone or together—can reduce
the intensity of tremors, typically by about half. Wrist-
strengthening exercises can also help stabilize the hand, making
it easier to write. In addition, try to avoid caffeine, certain asthma
medications, oral decongestants, and stress, all of which can
make the tremor worse.

### SHOULD I HAVE MY HEAD EXAMINED?

**Q** *I recently fell and hit my head while ice skating. I didn't
black out, see stars, or have any other symptoms except for
feeling slightly woozy for many days. Should I have gone to the
emergency room?*

**A** Generally, that's necessary only if a minor blow to the head
causes any of the following problems: a visible wound; classic
signs of concussion, including loss of consciousness, disturbed vision, headache, stiff neck, nausea, confusion, or unsteady gait; or
any symptoms that worsen in the days after the fall. In such cases a
doctor will test your memory, concentration, and coordination, any
of which may be impaired if the brain is damaged. Questionable

findings may warrant a closer look with a CT scan or an MRI. Both exams can reveal signs of bleeding in the brain, which may require surgical drainage. (Resist taking anything but acetaminophen to squelch pain; aspirin, ibuprofen, and other anti-inflammatory drugs can increase bleeding and mask certain worsening symptoms.) Note that you're not out of the woods for 8 to 12 weeks. During that time, blood can collect under the covering of the brain, causing subtle symptoms such as balance problems or involuntary hand or foot movements. If so, drainage would also be required.

## TREATING A TREMOR

**Q** *Are there any vitamins, minerals, or specific foods that might help the condition known as "benign essential tremor"?*

**A** The medical term "essential" is often applied to conditions for which the cause is not known, and that unfortunately is the case with this troublesome neurological ailment. It sometimes runs in families, so there may be a genetic component. Unfortunately, there is no convincing evidence that any nutritional therapy will improve this trembling of the hands, face, or voice. Small quantities of alcohol may temporarily suppress it, and beta-blocker drugs (such as propranolol or nadolol) frequently help. The anticonvulsant primidone *(Mysoline)* is also effective in some patients. In addition, one study with a small number of patients found about half responded well to a drug called methazolamide *(Neptazane),* also used for glaucoma. However, those medications help the tremor only as long as they're being used. It may be more helpful to minimize intake of substances that can worsen tremors, such as caffeine, certain drugs for asthma, and oral decongestants.

## SCIATICA AND NUMB TOES

**Q** Last year I had sciatica from my back down to my right leg. The pain cleared up but left me with a kind of numbness in three toes (big toe and adjacent two) that I can't seem to shake. What can I do about this?

**A** Your numbness probably stems from some chronic irritation of the sciatic nerve root as it leaves the spinal cord. This may be caused by a herniated, or "slipped," disk, a disk fragment, or a bone spur. Unfortunately, the longer the numbness lasts, the less likely it is to disappear. A consultation with a neurologist would be advisable.

## SLAPPING GAIT

**Q** What are the cause and treatment of "slap foot," which makes the front of the foot slap down noisily when walking?

**A** Slap foot, or what doctors call a slapping gait, results when something goes wrong with the nerves controlling the muscles in front of the lower leg. The weakened muscles can't lift the forefoot, which hits the ground before the heel. The problem could be caused by a bulging or herniated intervertebral disk or a bone spur pressing on the spinal cord. It could also be caused by a damaged or inflamed nerve supplying the front part of the leg. Treatment depends on identifying the cause. If no treatment is effective, a brace can be helpful.

---

┌─────────────────────────┐
│  ✚ *Office* **Visit**   │
└─────────────────────────┘

# RESTLESS LEGS SYNDROME: CAN YOU WALK AWAY FROM IT?

NOT LONG AGO, AN 80-YEAR-OLD retired TV executive told me about an affliction that has plagued him for decades. Since his early 50s, he has experienced involuntary leg movements that invariably come on in the evening as he settles back to watch TV, read, or enjoy a movie or play. He found that the only way to stop the spasmodic jerking was to get up and walk. The jerking also sometimes happened at night after he'd fallen asleep—but never during the day.

His symptoms are fairly typical of a widespread condition called restless legs syndrome (RLS). Often mischaracterized by doctors as a psychological aberration, RLS is actually a neurologic disorder that affects as many as 15 percent of all Americans. Besides causing involuntary leg movements, RLS commonly triggers a "creepy crawly" sensation in the legs that strikes mainly at night. Many RLS sufferers end up walking the floor well into the wee hours to shake the discomfort. As a result, they routinely suffer from sleep deprivation that can compromise their productivity and quality of life.

Doctors have known about RLS for more than 50 years, but it's only within the past few years that diagnostic guidelines have been established and promising therapies have come along.

Alert your physician if you notice these RLS hallmarks:

• Vague, nonpainful sensations in the legs that cause involuntary movements in the toes, feet, or legs while awake or asleep.

• Symptoms that are worse when you're at rest especially in the evening or at night and that are relieved by walking or other physical activity.

## MEDICATION SOLUTIONS

Although the underlying cause of RLS remains unknown, there's reason to believe that the disorder may stem from a deficiency of dopamine, a chemical that helps transmit signals in the brain. RLS symptoms can be relieved by drugs that compensate for that dopamine deficit. Those dopaminergic agents come in two types:

• Medications that boost dopamine levels. These drugs, which include the oral medication carbidopa-levodopa *(Sinemet, Sinemet CR),* can help relieve nighttime leg discomfort and involuntary leg movements. But *Sinemet* also causes most patients to experience "augmentation," in which RLS symptoms shift to earlier in the day, intensify, or migrate to the upper body.

• Dopamine-receptor agonists. These drugs, which include pergolide *(Permax),* pramipexole *(Mirapex),* and ropinirole *(Requip),* mimic dopamine's ability to turn on the brain's dopamine receptors. Recent controlled trials have shown pergolide and pramipexole to be effective against RLS. Moreover, only 10 to 15 percent of patients on pergolide experience augmentation, vs. about 80 percent on *Sinemet.* But dopamine-receptor agonists can trigger side effects—such as headaches, nausea, and vomiting—that sometimes limit their use.

Other categories of drugs may help as well. Benzodiazepines such as clonazepam *(Klonopin)* taken at bedtime can allay nighttime symptoms. More-severe cases may require clonazepam in combination with a dopaminergic agent. Anticonvulsants, such as gabapentin *(Neurontin),* have also shown promise at relieving RLS symptoms in some patients.

## OTHER TRIGGERS AND THERAPIES

Certain medical disorders can trigger RLS: iron deficiency; peripheral neuropathies as caused by diabetes, rheumatoid arthritis, or vitamin-B12 deficiency. RLS symptoms may improve or disappear when such underlying disorders are treated. RLS can also be brought on by certain drugs, including antidepressants, calcium-channel blockers, beta-blockers, histamine blockers, metoclopramide *(Reglan),* lithium, and phenytoin *(Dilantin).* In those instances, stopping the drug can improve or cure the disorder. Avoid alcohol and caffeine.

Nondrug therapies—such as physical therapy, water therapy, massage, and vibratory or electrical stimulation—have not worked with any consistency.

## Nose, mouth, and throat disorders

### SORE-THROAT SOLUTIONS

**Q** *Every couple of years I develop a bad sore throat and I take the antibiotics my doctor prescribes. Am I doing the right thing?*

**A** That depends. It's appropriate if streptococcal bacteria are causing the soreness. You probably have strep if your throat is deep red with white patches, you have a fever that started suddenly, and the lymph nodes in your neck are painfully enlarged. If the infection isn't causing major discomfort and doesn't seem to be serious, wait for your doctor to confirm strep throat by taking a throat culture. But antibiotics won't help and may harm if a virus is the culprit. That's likely if you have other cold or flu symptoms such as a stuffy or runny nose or sneezing. While viral infections generally resolve on their own, see your doctor if the soreness lasts more than three days. If you experience extreme fatigue, difficulty opening your mouth, or severe difficulty swallowing, seek help immediately; you may have an abscess.

Whatever the cause, you can soothe your throat by sucking on cough drops, gargling with warm saltwater, eating ice cream or ice pops, drinking lots of fluids, humidifying dry air, and using throat sprays containing dyclonine *(Cepacol Maximum Strength Sore Throat Spray, Sucrets Throat Spray)* or phenol *(Cheracol Sore Throat Spray)*.

## EXTINGUISH BURNING MOUTH

**Q** *I'm a 45-year-old woman recently diagnosed with "burning mouth syndrome." Chewing gum eases the discomfort a little, and taking the drug nortriptyline helps somewhat more, but the pain in my mouth soon returns. What are the possible causes and cures?*

**A** Though the exact cause often remains a mystery, that syndrome—a persistent burning sensation with no visible irritation—sometimes results from the dry mouth occasionally associated with menopause. Chewing gum can help by stimulating saliva flow. Estrogen replacement therapy may also help restore the flow, but a burning mouth shouldn't be the only reason for taking the hormone. If estrogen therapy isn't an option, low doses of the anticonvulsant clonazepam *(Klonopin)* can usually reduce the discomfort, by stimulating the release of pain-suppressing chemicals in the brain—although clonazepam itself sometimes adds to the dryness. When antidepressants such as nortriptyline *(Pamelor)* help, psychological factors may be contributing to the syndrome. However, antidepressants may also dry the mouth; moreover, studies indicate that counseling reduces the pain more effectively than those drugs. Lastly, your doctor should check for underlying diseases or nutritional deficiencies that may occasionally spark a burning mouth.

## TOO MUCH SALIVA

**Q** *I salivate so much that the saliva chokes me when I try to sleep. My doctor hasn't been able to help. What could the problem be?*

**A** It's possible that you just have trouble swallowing. That problem, which people often don't notice, can cause saliva to collect in your mouth, making you think your saliva glands are working overtime. An ear, nose, and throat specialist can test your swallowing reflex, which can be damaged by several neurologic or muscular disorders. If the reflex is normal, you should probably see a dentist who specializes in salivary-gland disorders—usually at a university medical center or large hospital—who can measure your saliva secretion. If excessive salivation is the problem, doctors should check for an underlying cause, such as a drug side effect, gastroesophageal reflux, or a rare effect of diabetes.

## TOPOGRAPHICAL TONGUE

**Q** *I have intermittent bouts of "geographica lingua," in which my tongue sheds tissue, creating deep grooves that make eating uncomfortable. What causes this and what can I do about it?*

**A** Unfortunately, the cause and cure are both unknown. But you may be able to ease the mild discomfort of this otherwise harmless, relatively uncommon condition. Since the grooves tend to develop around points of irritation, avoid brushing your tongue or moving it around excessively. And have your dentist smooth any rough or sharp edges on your teeth and fix any ill-fitting dental appliances.

## DOUSING DRY MOUTH

**Q** *I'm a 63-year-old woman who takes a daily multivitamin for general health, omeprazole* (Prilosec) *for heartburn, and estrogen* (Premarin) *to relieve symptoms of menopause. Though I'm in good overall health and don't drink alcohol or smoke, I suffer from severe, chronic dry mouth. My dentist doesn't know what's causing it or how I could moisten my mouth. Do you?*

**A** This common condition is usually a side effect of drug therapy. Omeprazole sometimes does interfere with salivation—especially at high doses. So ask your doctor if you could try a lower dosage or switch to another medication to ease your heartburn without drying your mouth. The underlying cause could also be a medical condition such as Sjogren's syndrome, an often-undiagnosed autoimmune disorder, or one of several salivary-gland or neurological diseases.

If the cause can't be determined, treated, or modified, try stimulating your salivary glands by eating strong-tasting or fibrous foods (such as carrots and celery), sucking on sugar-free hard candy, or chewing sugar-free gum. (Since the saliva shortage raises the risk of cavities, limit your sugar intake and exercise good dental hygiene.) Sipping liquid frequently, sucking on ice cubes or sugar-free Popsicles, breathing through your nose, and using a humidifier can further help keep your mouth moist. If those steps fail, an over-the-counter saliva substitute *(Moi-Stir, Mouthkote, Optimoist, Salivart)* can provide short-term relief, and the prescription drug pilocarpine *(Salagen)* may increase saliva output (though it's not suitable for people with certain chronic diseases).

## OVERREACTIVE NOSE

**Q** *After enduring a stuffy nose for almost a year, I was diagnosed with vasomotor rhinitis, a nonallergic condition. My allergist told me that anger can aggravate it, but there's no cure. Is that true?*

**A** Yes. This common condition occurs when blood vessels in the nose overreact to certain environmental or emotional stimuli by swelling up and triggering excess mucus production. Common culprits include changes in air temperature and humidity, strong odors, spicy food, and even strong feelings like anger. If you can identify the triggers, you may be able to neutralize or avoid them. Exercising and keeping a hostility diary, for example, may curb anger. Although drugs cannot completely relieve symptoms, your doctor may prescribe an oral decongestant, an antihistamine, or a steroid nasal spray that can provide limited relief. Avoid over-the-counter decongestant nasal sprays, such as *Afrin* or *Otrivin,* which can actually make matters worse.

---

## COLD-SORE CURE?

**Q** *A popular magazine has been touting the use of lysine to prevent or lessen cold sores. What does your research say about this?*

**A** Studies have yet to prove that this amino acid can prevent the recurrence or speed the healing of cold sores. The few trials that have been conducted have not shown it to be helpful. There are, however, several steps that can help. First, try to avoid likely cold-sore triggers such as stress, windburn, excessive sun exposure, fatigue, or skin trauma around the lips, due to shaving, for example. Docosanol cream *(Abreva),* recently approved by the

Food and Drug Administration and available without a prescription, can accelerate healing. So can prescription acyclovir pills *(Zovirax)*, if taken early. (Acyclovir cream doesn't seem to help.) Other over-the-counter products such as anesthetic skin creams containing benzocaine *(Orajel)* or dibucaine *(Nupercainal)* or pain relievers such as acetaminophen *(Tylenol)* or ibuprofen *(Advil)* will not help the sores heal but can ease the discomfort. No matter what treatment you use, contact your doctor if the sores do not heal within 14 days. If you have more than six outbreaks a year, ask your doctor about taking acyclovir regularly, which can reduce the number of episodes by up to 80 percent.

## THRUSH

*Q A few months ago I developed "thrush"—whitish patches on my tongue and on the back of my throat—after a six-day course of intravenous antibiotics. The antibiotics apparently killed the normal protective bacteria in my mouth, allowing the thrush to develop. Now I'm concerned about my intestinal bacteria as well. So I've been taking L. acidophilus and bifidus supplements to reestablish those bacteria. Is that the right thing to do?*

*A* No. The bacterial imbalance that follows use of antibiotics may indeed allow other bacteria or fungi to take hold. Those include the candida that cause thrush. But while the "intestinal flora" supplements you mention have shown some benefits at reducing antibiotic-associated diarrhea, they have not been shown to be very effective at treating thrush. You should treat the candida with an effective antifungal medicine, such as oral fluconazole *(Diflucan)* or nystatin *(Mycostatin)*. The usual bacterial population will return to your mouth and intestinal tract on its own.

## NOSEBLEEDS

*Q* *I've had allergies since I was a child. Four years ago, I had an operation for a broken nose. Now my nose bleeds if I happen to rub it—even only gently. Why?*

*A* The problem probably has nothing to do with your broken nose or operation. But it may be related to your allergies—or, more precisely, your allergy medications. Antihistamines and decongestants can dry the mucous lining of the nasal passages. Rubbing, scratching, or other trauma can easily cause bleeding in a dry nose. To lessen drying, minimize your use of those medications and keep your environment comfortably humidified.

---

## SMELL LOSS

*Q* *I'm 83 years old and seem to be losing my ability to smell. My doctor says I should travel nearly 100 miles for special smell tests. Is loss of smell really such a significant problem?*

*A* It might be, since it could affect your health and safety. You may be unable to detect smoke or gas in your home or realize when food has spoiled. And your nose is largely responsible for your sense of taste. Loss of taste could cause you to use excessive salt or sugar in hopes of increasing flavor, or to lose interest in eating entirely. And it could signal an underlying disorder such as vitamin-B12 or folic-acid deficiency, hypothyroidism, diabetes, Parkinson's disease, stroke, or a brain tumor.

But you probably don't have to take special tests to evaluate your loss of smell. Instead, you can confirm it at home: Close your eyes and see if you can distinguish chocolate ice cream from vanilla, or one jelly-bean flavor from another. Or douse a cloth with alcohol and see if you can smell it while slowly bringing the cloth from your chest up to your nose.

If you flunk those tests, or if food seems generally tasteless, ask your doctor to rule out any underlying medical problems. Loss of smell could also be a medication side effect; if so, adjusting the dosage or switching to a different drug can help.

If the problem persists, be extra careful about turning off the gas range, have someone check for gas leaks and food spoilage, and make sure your home has functioning gas and smoke detectors. Choosing spicy flavors and interesting textures can help keep food tasty.

## POSTNASAL DRIP

**Q** *I suffer from postnasal drip, which constantly fills my throat with phlegm. What can I do about it?*

**A** Probably not much. Postnasal drip is typically caused by air pollution, allergies, or infections. The irritated membranes in your nose and sinuses thicken and produce too much mucus. When the condition becomes chronic, it's often difficult to tell what caused it. And it's seldom cured.

Side effects from the standard medications used for postnasal drip—antibiotics, antihistamines, and decongestants—often outweigh their meager benefits. If you should try those drugs and they don't work, see an otorhinolaryngologist (ear, nose, and throat specialist). Once cysts, polyps, and tumors have been ruled out, either a corticosteroid nasal spray or cortisone injections into the nasal membranes may help.

## LOSS OF TASTE AND SMELL

**Q** *At the age of 54, I seem to be losing my sense of taste and smell. What might be causing this?*

**A** Like hearing and vision, taste and smell tend to deteriorate with age. In addition, various illnesses and injuries can damage the nerves connecting the sense organs to the brain. Loss of smell, for example, can be caused by nasal or sinus infections, nasal polyps, meningitis, or brain tumors. Loss of smell can affect taste. So can allergies, tongue injuries, stroke, or tumors. You should consult your physician to rule out possible underlying disorders.

---

## RECURRENT SINUS INFECTIONS

**Q** *What can I do about recurrent sinus infections? They clear up temporarily after antibiotics, but return in a couple of months. My doctor says X-rays show thickening in my sinuses.*

**A** That thickening is due to chronic inflammation of the sinus lining. And an inflamed lining secretes excessive amounts of mucus, which predisposes you to yet another infection. You may need aggressive treatment with longer courses of antibiotics to break the cycle. Failing that, you should be evaluated by an otorhinolaryngologist (ear, nose, and throat specialist) for possible surgery to permit better drainage.

---

## ✚ *Office* **Visit**

# A TOUGH ONE TO SWALLOW

"I THOUGHT IT WAS ABOUT TIME I looked into this," said a 49-year-old politician, an infrequent seeker of medical attention. His complaint of pain while swallowing had been present on and off for a number of years. "Since it mostly bothered me during campaign time, especially at fund-raising affairs when I had to make after-dinner speeches, I never thought it was important enough to mention; probably just tension and stress." But some publicity about cancer of the esophagus raised his medical consciousness enough to make him schedule an office visit.

Swallowing is a natural action that we perform over a hundred times a day without giving it a second thought, but it's actually a complicated maneuver involving the coordinated actions of nerves and muscles of the tongue, throat, and esophagus. When everything is working right, people can swallow even while standing on their heads, but even a minor glitch in any of those systems can throw the process off enough for them to notice.

Discomfort, disability, or pain during the act of swallowing (dysphagia), especially when persistent or recurrent, should be brought to medical attention because it almost always signifies some abnormality. The question is: Which one?

## FINDING A CAUSE

Difficulty in starting the swallowing process arises from damage to the nerves and muscles in the back of the throat. A stroke is the most common cause but is usually accompanied by other symptoms, such as weakness in an arm or leg. My patient had no symptoms suggestive of a stroke, and besides, stroke-related swallowing problems don't usually produce the pain that he complained of.

Nor, after listening carefully to his story, did I think he had esophageal cancer, the concern that had led him to my office in the first place. Dysphagia caused by this usually aggressive malignancy gets rapidly worse and is invariably accompanied by weight loss. His symptoms were intermittent and hadn't gotten any worse over several years.

He didn't have heartburn, often caused by the reflux of stomach acid up into the esophagus. Chronic acid reflux can irritate or ulcerate the esophagus enough to interfere with swallowing. Besides, he had already tried myriad over-the-counter antacid pills and liquids, none of which had done him any good. If he had had heartburn, those should have at least moderated his symptoms.

He didn't take any of the medications known to produce a little-known condition called "pill dysphagia," difficulty in swallowing due to drugs capable of causing inflammation and eventual narrowing or stricture of the lower esophagus. Most cases of pill dysphagia arise from antibiotics, notably doxycycline *(Vibramycin)*. Other pills commonly involved in pill dysphagia are potassium tablets, aspirin, and nonsteroidal anti-inflammatory medications such as ibuprofen *(Advil, Motrin)*, corticosteroids such as prednisone *(Deltasone, Orasone)*, and the heart drug quinidine *(Cardioquin)*.

Finally, there was nothing in his history to suggest that he had infectious esophagitis. This inflammation of the esophagus is usually caused by a fungal infection in someone whose immune system has been compromised, for example by immunosuppressive drugs (after, say, a kidney transplant), HIV infection, or a prolonged course of antibiotics or corticosteroids. He didn't fit into any of those categories.

## PROBLEM SOLVED

I referred our politician to a gastroenterology colleague, who performed an upper endoscopy, in which the esophagus is viewed through a flexible lighted tube inserted into the mouth and then threaded into the esophagus. In the lower-most part of the esophagus, he saw a ring-shaped web of the esophageal lining projecting into the passageway.

This proved to be a Schatzki's ring: a benign, fleshy protrusion capable of retarding the passage of solid foods from the lower end of the esophagus into the stomach. Believed by some to be congenital, a Schatzski's ring can produce obstructive symptoms such as pain or discomfort while swallowing solid food, particularly meat (hence its nickname: "steakhouse syndrome"). The condition occurs in about 15 percent of people but causes symptoms in relatively few. No one knows why the symptoms come and go and show up only in later life—but they match my patient's story exactly.

The treatment was simple and immediate. At the same sitting, while the patient was still sedated, the gastroenterologist inserted a dilator tube that broke the web. That was more than two years ago, and the dysphagia has not returned.

## Parenting and pregnancy

### BUCKLE UP IF YOU'RE PREGNANT

**Q** *Is it safe for a woman to wear a safety belt while pregnant?*

**A** Yes. Studies have found that a properly worn safety belt not only helps protect the expectant mother during a car accident but also dramatically reduces the likelihood of harm to the fetus. Pregnant women using safety belts are half as likely as their unrestrained counterparts to go into premature labor or deliver a low-birthweight baby after an accident. The lower belt should fit under the woman's belly and snugly across her lap, with the upper portion running between her breasts. Whenever possible, pregnant women should ride as passengers, to avoid possible contact with the steering wheel during an accident. And everyone should leave airbags operational and keep their seat as far away as comfortably possible from the dashboard or steering wheel.

### BREAST-FEEDING AND BRITTLE BONES

**Q** *In December you said that breast-feeding may reduce the mother's risk of osteoporosis. Why is that? Doesn't secreting the milk cause a loss of calcium?*

**A** Yes it does. As a result, bone density typically does decline during the breast-feeding months. However, studies have found that breast-feeding does not increase the mother's risk of thin bones and fractures in later life. And, in fact, some studies show that breast-feeding actually decreases the risk. That's probably because calcium absorption from dietary sources increases after breast-feeding stops; as a result, women quickly regain the lost bone and wind up with even more than they had before.

## POST-PILL PREGNANCY

*Is it true that a woman should wait three months after discontinuing birth-control pills before getting pregnant? If so, why?*

It's a good idea to hold off trying to conceive for at least a month or two, to allow time for your menstrual periods to become regular. Irregular periods make it harder to detect ovulation and to determine your due date when you do become pregnant. However, we know of no evidence that becoming pregnant immediately after discontinuing birth-control pills causes harm to mother or child.

## POSTPARTUM DEPRESSION

*What causes postpartum depression? What are the latest treatments?*

Postpartum depression—not the more common postpartum "blues"—is a psychiatric disorder that can severely impair day-to-day functioning. Its onset is usually within the first few weeks or months after childbirth. A woman who has once had postpartum depression can experience it again after future births.

The causes of postpartum depression are not well understood. The sudden change from the pregnant state, with accompanying changes in hormone levels, probably plays some role. Occasionally postpartum depression can be part of a temporary inflammatory thyroid disease called thyroiditis.

In contrast to the self-limited "blues," which usually lasts only a short time and needs only emotional support, true postpartum depression requires the attention of a psychiatrist. Antidepressant medications can help. Rarely, electroconvulsive (electric shock) therapy may be necessary.

---

## ILLICIT DRUGS: PREGNANCY PERIL?

**Q** *Ten years ago, in college, I experimented with several drugs, including marijuana, cocaine, and LSD. Now I'm 30 and my husband and I are thinking about starting a family. Have I done any permanent damage to my egg supply? Is the risk of birth defects increased?*

**A** Go ahead and start your family. With the exception of certain anticancer medications, prior drug use, by males or females, does not appear to have any lasting effects on reproduction.

---

# Respiratory infections

## WHERE THERE'S SMOKE

**Q** *A year or so ago I was diagnosed as having a bronchial infection caused by Hemophilus influenza bacteria. Despite
having taken three or four antibiotics, I still have a very produc-
tive cough. Could the fact that I smoke cigarettes be hampering
my recovery?*

**A** Very likely. Not only do smokers experience more respiratory infections than nonsmokers do, but they also are likely
to have more difficulty recovering. Smoking destroys cilia, the
tiny filaments that help to move infected mucus up and out of the
lungs. And the ability of the lungs to repair tissue damage is impaired by years of smoking.

---

## ANTIBIOTICS FOR A BAD COLD

**Q** *I've had two particularly bad colds over the past year. Both
times, my doctor prescribed antibiotics. I thought that a
cold is a viral infection and that antibiotics aren't effective against
viruses. Why the antibiotics?*

**A** That depends. Antibiotics indeed won't do anything for a
viral infection such as the common cold. But sometimes a
cold virus leads to a bacterial infection in the sinus or bronchial
airways, which does require antibiotics. Sinus infections can produce a thick, yellow or deeply colored discharge from the nose,
tenderness or pain just above or below the eyes, and mild fever.
Bronchial infections can also cause fever as well as a cough that

brings up greenish yellow sputum or even some blood.

If you have none of those symptoms, you shouldn't take antibiotics. The drugs can cause such side effects as nausea, diarrhea, and rashes. They can also kill off the body's own protective bacteria, allowing fungal infections to grow, and inappropriate use can add to the growing problem of antibiotic-resistant germs.

## Skin care

### DARK PATCHES OF SKIN

**Q** *I'm a 63-year-old woman with several dark brown patches of skin on my face that won't go away. Is there some cream or lotion that can lighten or remove them?*

**A** Some treatments may lighten them but probably won't remove them. The most likely cause of that darkening is overproduction of pigment by skin cells—usually triggered by increased levels of the hormone estrogen during pregnancy or while taking oral contraceptives or hormone-replacement therapy. But your doctor should also rule out other possible causes, such as an allergic reaction to a drug, including certain antibiotics, antiseizure and psychiatric drugs, and diuretics; and underlying conditions such as hyperthyroidism and certain nutritional deficiencies. Stopping an offending drug or treating an underlying condition probably won't cause the patches to fade, but they may be lightened somewhat by using a nonprescription bleaching cream containing hydroquinone *(Black & White Bleaching Cream, Esoterica)*, either alone or together with a prescription exfoliating cream such as azelaic acid *(Azelex)* or tretinoin *(Renova)*. Sunshine encourages the darkening, and those treatments can make you extra sensitive to sunlight, so wear sunscreen whenever you're exposed to the sun.

---

## TOPICAL NAIL-FUNGUS CURE?

**Q** *In your recent story on hair and nails you discuss systemic drugs for nail infections but don't mention topical treatments. Why not?*

**A** Because they're not very effective. Prescription topical drugs such as ciclopirox *(Penlac Nail Lacquer)* and naftifine *(Naftin)* are generally much safer than systemic ones. But they need to be applied twice a day for 4 to 6 months on fingernails, 12 to 18 months on toenails. Even then, they quell only about 10 percent of infections. There are no nonprescription topical-drug options. Preliminary evidence suggests that one herbal product, tea-tree oil, might work slightly better than the prescription topicals—but that's not saying much. In one six-month study, for example, applying the oil twice a day and periodically filing the infected toenail killed the fungus in nearly 20 percent of patients; there was no follow-up on whether the infection recurred, as it often does.

---

## DO SUNSCREENS EXPIRE?

**Q** *Should I throw away the tubes of sunscreen that have been sitting in my medicine cabinet for several years?*

**A** Most likely. Sunscreens eventually start losing their sun-protecting power when the ingredients start to separate.

That generally happens after the expiration date, which should be printed on the label; it's usually two to three years after the product was made. Toss out any sunscreen that has expired or shows signs of separating, such as grittiness or changed appearance.

## SOOTHING SCALP ITCH

**Q** *My scalp itches all the time, but I don't have a lot of dandruff. What could cause this condition?*

**A** Many things, but it's most likely an inflammatory skin condition, such as seborrhea or mild psoriasis. While the causes and cures of those conditions remain unknown, symptoms such as itching and mild flaking can be soothed with shampoos containing tar *(Denorex, Neutrogena T/Gel)* or salicylic acid *(Neutrogena T/Sal, Scalpicin),* or with hydrocortisone scalp lotion *(Neutrogena T/Scalp).* If those measures fail to bring relief within a week or two, see your doctor, who can rule out rarer, but often more serious, underlying conditions and can prescribe a more potent corticosteroid lotion.

## MANICURES AND NAIL INFECTIONS

**Q** *My nail salon uses the same set of tools on many different clients, disinfecting them between jobs. Is that enough to avoid spreading infections, or should I choose a salon that provides a separate set of tools for each client?*

**A** That depends on how well they're cleaned. Most salons meticulously eliminate the risk of transmitting infection by properly sterilizing with either steam or a chemical disinfectant. If a salon is licensed and looks clean, and the technicians are fastidious, you probably don't have to worry. If you're unsure, ask about sterilization methods (an establishment that takes infection control seriously should be eager to tell you about it). If you're still skeptical, bring your own tools or find a salon that offers each client a separate set. Regardless of the tools used, avoid having your cuticles trimmed since that can promote infection. And contact your physician if your fingers burn, itch, sting, or turn red after a manicure—all signs of possible infection or allergic reaction.

## STUB OUT TOENAIL FUNGUS?

**Q** *Is there any cure for the fungus that's deforming my toenails?*

**A** Yes—but the cure could be worse than the infection, which may not require treatment at all. The oral drugs itraconazole *(Sporanox)* and terbinafine *(Lamisil)* will usually eradicate the fungus. But liver damage is a rare side effect of both drugs, and itraconazole has caused a few cases of heart failure. Alternatively, your doctor could prescribe another antifungal, fluconazole *(Diflucan)*, which hasn't been approved by the Food and Drug Administration for treating toenails but appears to be effective and somewhat safer than the other two. All three drugs can cause other, milder side effects and may interact with several medications. And they're expensive.

Fortunately, while the fungus thickens, roughens, and discolors the nails, it usually causes no discomfort. And while the untreated infection almost always persists, it rarely spreads or gets worse. So it's generally best to forgo treatment if you can live with the condition.

## SKIN SPOTS

**Q** *I have white spots on the skin of my neck and both hands. I'm embarrassed to be seen in public with this condition, and I've tried skin dyes, but they don't work well. What are these spots, and will anything make them go away?*

**A** Those spots are the hallmark of vitiligo, a relatively common disorder that destroys pigment cells in the skin. In addition to skin dyes, there are treatments that aim to restore some of the skin's color by stimulating any remaining pigment cells. The usual technique uses topical drugs called psoralens followed by exposure to ultraviolet (UV) light. Unfortunately, that technique works only about half the time and may cause bothersome side effects, such as increased sensitivity to sunlight as well as headaches and nausea. A new laser therapy introduced recently at a meeting of the American Academy of Dermatology has shown promising results in as few as six treatments—compared with a minimum of 100 drug-plus-UV treatments—with milder side effects. This treatment may become available in a year or so.

---

## PSORIASIS RELIEF

**Q** *Our daughter suffers from severe psoriasis. Can you suggest any effective treatments?*

**A** Unfortunately there's no cure for this common condition. And no one knows what causes the skin to start shedding so rapidly that it creates thick, itchy, inflamed, scaly patches.

Avoiding alcohol, cigarettes, stress, and sunburn and keeping the skin moist can help prevent flare-ups. Medicinal creams and ointments, such as tar *(Estar, Psorigel)*, calcipotriene *(Dovonex)*, and tazarotene *(Tazorac)*, can often help as well. But severe cases require stronger therapy. The first option is usually ultraviolet light, either UVB alone or UVA plus drugs called psoralens (a combination known as PUVA); such treatment can help keep psoriasis in remission. When flare-ups occur, the drugs acitretin *(Soriatane)*, cyclosporine *(Sandimmune)*, and methotrexate *(Rheumatrex)* can reduce their severity and duration. But those drugs can have severe side effects, and cyclosporine's potential toxicity limits its use to short periods only. In the toughest cases, UVB or PUVA can be combined with acitretin or methotrexate.

There's also a promising new option that's been submitted to the FDA for review. A preliminary study found that taking the drug alefacept *(Amevive)* for 12 weeks reduced symptoms by at least 75 percent in one-third of patients with chronic psoriasis. And the relief lasted for at least three months after they stopped taking the drug.

---

## ANTIWRINKLE WORKOUT?

**Q** *I've heard that facial exercises are useless for reducing wrinkles. But what about exercises designed to tone the muscles of the neck and lower jaw to prevent or minimize double chin and so-called turkey neck? Are they equally futile?*

**A** Yes. While a face or jaw workout might tone some muscles, flabby facial muscles aren't a significant cause of sagging skin. The main problem is weakening or damage to the skin itself, caused by heredity, aging, and sun damage. Facial exercises won't counteract the loss of elasticity and fat that leads to skin thinning and drooping. In fact the repeated stretching involved may even worsen the sagging.

---

## BAGS UNDER THE EYES

**Q** *What causes bags under the eyes, and can anything help remove them?*

**A** As the skin and muscles under the eyes weaken with age, they start to sag and to allow fluid or fat to build up behind them, creating bags. However, many other factors can cause under-eye bags. Temporary ones, for example, could stem from lack of sleep; an allergic reaction to a drug, cosmetic, or environmental irritant; or water retention due to menstruation or pregnancy. Persistent fluid-filled bags can signal a more serious problem, such as thyroid, kidney, liver, or heart disease, all of which can cause water retention. If a physician confirms that tired facial tissue is the culprit, the only means of permanently unpacking the bags is a surgical procedure called blepharoplasty, in which excess skin, muscle, and fat are removed through small incisions.

## ITCHING ALL OVER

**Q** *For the past two years, I've itched from my scalp to the soles of my feet, including the palms of my hands, my ears, and my eyes. There is no rash. At night the itching is accompanied by muscular spasms in my legs and a burning sensation.*

**A** Persistent itching can be caused by allergies to food or medications and by skin disorders such as scabies (which don't always have visible signs). The burning sensation you've experienced could be a sign of nerve inflammation. A physical exam is needed to find the cause of your itching. If your physician can find no treatable cause, he or she may recommend an oral antihistamine to relieve the symptoms.

## SCRATCHING AN ITCH

**Q** *For months I've been suffering from an annoying itch. It starts in one spot, I scratch it, and it turns red and bumpy. Then it disappears and starts up again somewhere else. I've been taking an antihistamine, which helps, but I'm worried. What's wrong with me?*

**A** The red, bumpy rashes you describe are probably the result of scratching, not the cause of the itch. Unexplained generalized itching, called pruritus, has several possible causes. Older people often itch in the winter because their skin becomes drier. Using water-soluble lubricating oils, bathing less frequently, and running a room humidifier may help. Certain systemic diseases, such as diabetes, liver disease, and some forms of cancer, can also cause itching. These can easily be excluded by appropriate tests. If the cause is unknown, antihistamines, such as hydroxyzine *(Atarax, Vistaril),* may help.

---

## SHINGLES: THE AFTEREFFECTS

**Q** *About a year ago, my wife contracted a severe case of shingles. Although the rash is gone now, the severe pain persists. Her doctors have prescribed only pain-relief pills. Is there a permanent cure?*

**A** The pain that remains after an attack of shingles is known as postherpetic neuralgia, and it is notoriously hard to vanquish. Some drugs have proved helpful, but not for all people. They include capsaicin (often sold as *Zostrix),* a topical medication; amitriptyline *(Elavil),* an antidepressant; phenytoin *(Dilantin),* carbamazepine *(Tegretol),* or gabapentin *(Neurontin),* anticonvulsants; injections of corticosteroids; and lidocaine skin patches. In other people, only time brings relief; the pain can last for months or years.

Some dermatologists prescribe oral cortisone, taken for three weeks after shingles first appears, to prevent the pain that persists after an attack. But the efficacy of this particular treatment remains unproven.

## FAREWELL TO KELOID SCARS

**Q** *I've had keloids on my chest for 25 years and they seem to get thicker and more itchy each day. I've had them removed by both conventional and laser surgery and injected with cortisone, but they always come back. Can anything more be done?*

**A** Keloids are thick, raised, ropy scars that can occur after a surgical procedure or accidental laceration. The tendency to develop keloids appears to be hereditary. In certain people—particularly African-Americans, Asians, and Hispanics—recurrence is common and hard to avoid. Treatment depends on both the size and location of the keloid and includes injection with corticosteroids, surgical removal, laser therapy, cryosurgery, and others. As with any disorder that has multiple treatments, no one particular method is good for all patients.

It's best to remove the keloid and immediately inject the area with cortisone. Additional injections should be given at the first sign of itching, which foreshadows the keloid's reappearance. Within two years, most keloids treated this way are permanently banished. Keloids that aren't bothersome in comfort or appearance can be safely left alone.

## SPOTTING SKIN CANCER

**Q** *Should a thorough inspection of the skin be part of a comprehensive physical examination?*

**A** Yes. Each year more than 1 million new cases of skin cancer are diagnosed in the United States, and more than 10,000 people die from the disease. Total body examinations are crucial for early detection and treatment of both skin cancers and premalignant skin lesions. Removal of the lesions usually results in a complete cure, especially if they are detected at an early stage. If your doctor fails to include a total body exam in your physical, ask for it. If you're at increased risk for skin cancer (because of previous cancerous lesions, family history, or fair complexion), you may want to consult a dermatologist for the exam.

## ROSACEA

**Q** *I have rosacea, mostly on my cheeks. What can I do about it?*

**A** In some people, avoiding hot or spicy foods, hot beverages, and alcohol will minimize this chronic blood-vessel inflammation, which appears as redness or pustules on the cheeks, nose, chin, forehead, or eyelids. If those measures don't help, your physician can prescribe oral or topical antibiotics that will control the condition. If that doesn't work, a doctor might prescribe metronidazole gel *(MetroGel)* for a particularly stubborn case. But avoid hydrocortisone cream; long-term use can cause changes that resemble rosacea itself.

## REMOVING BLACKHEADS

**Q** *What's the safest, most effective way to remove blackheads on the nose or elsewhere on the face?*

**A** If your blackheads are associated with facial acne, seek professional help because of the possibility of infection. For the occasional blackhead, first wash your face (and hands) with soap and warm water, then, using a blackhead remover, press down the skin around the blackhead to extrude the oxidized matter plugging the pore. Contrary to myth, this practice does no harm.

## HARRIED BY HIVES

**Q** *About a week ago I suddenly developed hives— blistery blotches on my skin that seem to appear and disappear within a short time. Why would hives wait until I was 67 years old before appearing? What could be causing them?*

**A** Hives can show up at any age. Unfortunately, their cause remains a mystery nearly to 70 percent of the time. Allergies to food, food additives, medication, or other ingested substances probably account for most cases. If the hives recur frequently, keeping a diary of your food and medication might provide a clue to the specific agent. Cold, heat, and even physical pressure can give some people hives as well. Anxiety and emotional upset are overrated as a cause of hives but can provoke an occasional outbreak. Whatever the cause, antihistamines can relieve the discomfort. Occasionally, temporary use of a prescription steroid medication such as prednisone may be necessary.

# ✚ *Office* **Visit**

# PSORIASIS, WITHOUT THE HEARTBREAK

"THE ITCHING CAN DRIVE YOU CRAZY," moaned a 46-year-old stock analyst with a decade-long history of severe psoriasis. "I'm in my dermatologist's office so often, I'm thinking of having my mail delivered there." While some people with psoriasis find it highly uncomfortable, others, such as my brother, a retired executive, hardly ever itch and seem to get along fine with nothing more than over-the-counter creams and ointments, sun exposure in the summer, and a wintertime vacation in the Caribbean.

Psoriasis is a benign, noncontagious disease characterized by red, slightly elevated patches with silvery scales and clearly delineated borders. Patches vary in size from pinpoint to huge maplike configurations covering large areas of the body; favored sites are elbows, genitals, and knees. The patches tend to bleed easily when scratched. The disease is often accompanied by pitting and deformities of the fingernails and toenails. Psoriatic arthritis, especially of the joint adjacent to the nails, can be painful and resistant to the usual anti-inflammatory drugs. There are about 7 million psoriasis patients in the U.S., with equal occurrence among men and women. It can appear at any age and seems to run in families.

Dermatologists have long known that psoriasis results when skin cells grow so abnormally fast that they don't have time to scale off normally, resulting in the buildup of the characteristic psoriatic plaques. More recently, advances in immunology have led to the finding that psoriasis most likely involves the overactivation of T-cells, a type of white blood cell, that in turn sends out chemical messengers, called cytokines, that inflame the skin and stimulate its overgrowth.

## MILD CASES, MILD TREATMENT

People with mild psoriasis do fine with the occasional use of over-the-counter hydrocortisone creams and regular exposure to sunlight, which has long been known to improve symptoms. (One treatment actually listed in medical textbooks is a trip to the Dead Sea, for exposure to its unique filtered below-sea-level ultraviolet light.)

Those with somewhat more extensive, though still moderate, disease can choose from an ever-growing array of effective topical treatments. Halobetasol *(Ultravate)* and clobetasol *(Temovate)* are but two examples of high-potency steroid creams or ointments that suppress the underlying inflammation. Calcipotriene *(Dovonex)* is a vitamin D analog that inhibits skin-cell growth. Its disadvantage is that it works very slowly, so it's usually applied in conjunction with a steroid cream. Tazarotene *(Tazorac)* is a retinoid (vitamin A derivative) that attacks both inflammation and skin-cell overgrowth.

## THE BIGGER GUNS

Some cases of psoriasis are so severe that they not only don't respond to those topical therapies, but spread to cover a third or more of a person's skin. For such cases, one effective treatment is phototherapy, exposure to UVB rays in a shower-size box in the dermatologist's office. The effect is enhanced by the administration of a photosensitizer, methoxsalen, taken by mouth two hours before exposure. Sometimes, this treatment is given in conjunction with a drug that suppresses the immune system, such as methotrexate or cyclosporin—though both those drugs can have significant side effects, including serious kidney or liver damage.

That's why there's much excitement over several biologic drugs for psoriasis that don't seem to pose the same risk. One of them, alefacept *(Amevive),* has already been approved by the Food and Drug Administration for treatment of moderate to severe psoriasis. Alefacept destroys activated T cells, thus stopping the psoriasis process early in its tracks.

Another biologic, etanercept *(Enbrel),* has been approved for the treatment of psoriatic arthritis (and rheumatoid arthritis), and is awaiting approval for psoriasis; it works by inactivating one of those cytokine messengers. Infliximab *(Remicade)* and efalizumab *(Raptiva),* each already approved for rheumatoid arthritis and Crohn's disease, have also been shown to be effective for psoriasis. Because these new biologics affect the immune system, long-term side effects are unknown. And they are very expensive.

My stock analyst's particularly stubborn case of psoriasis was resistant to phototherapy and methotrexate. He has been started on a three-month course of weekly injections of alefacept. Stay tuned.

## Stomach ailments

### ARTIFICIAL SUGAR AND BELLY PAIN

**Q** *After eating sugar-free jelly beans, my husband developed severe stomach cramps. Is there anything in sugar-free foods that could cause that problem?*

**A** Yes. Such foods are often sweetened with substances called sugar alcohols, which can cause stomach cramps and diarrhea. Those sweeteners appear on labels with such names as erythritol, lactitol, maltitol, mannitol, sorbitol, and xylitol. If you're sensitive to sugar alcohols, as little as 10 to 15 grams—the typical amount in one to two servings of sweetened food—can trigger gastrointestinal distress.

---

### GASTRITIS RELIEF

**Q** *I often have upper-abdominal pain stemming from gastritis. What causes that?*

**A** Anything that inflames the stomach lining can spark gastritis, a sometimes sharp but often dull, gnawing upper abdominal pain that can be accompanied by belching, bloating, and nausea. Heartburn may cause similar symptoms, but that pain typically is a burning sensation in the center of the chest, behind the breastbone. The three most common causes of stomach-lining inflammation are:

• Increased secretion of stomach acid, stimulated by coffee, tea, alcohol, or cigarettes.

• Direct irritation by a food such as hot peppers or by a medication, particularly a nonsteroidal anti-inflammatory drug

(NSAID) such as aspirin, ibuprofen *(Advil),* or naproxen *(Aleve).*

• Erosion of the stomach's mucus barrier, most often caused by prolonged use of NSAIDs.

You may be able to pacify the pain by avoiding those provoking substances and taking nonprescription heartburn drugs such as famotidine *(Pepcid AC)* or ranitidine *(Zantac 75).* If those measures fail, your doctor may prescribe a more potent acid-reducer such as lansoprazole *(Prevacid)* or omeprazole *(Prilosec).*

## WHEN TO TEST YOUR GUT FOR BUGS

**Q** *For several years I suffered from an ulcer. But it wasn't until I was tested for* H. pylori, *the* Helicobacter pylori *bacterium, that my doctor discovered I had an infection and needed antibiotics. When should people get tested for this bug?*

**A** Since *H. pylori* is quite common but usually harmless—causing ulcers in only 5 to 20 percent of infected people, and possibly contributing to stomach cancer in a much smaller fraction—testing is generally warranted in only two circumstances: if you have ulcers that can't be explained by the most common cause, regularly taking nonsteroidal anti-inflammatory drugs like aspirin or ibuprofen *(Advil, Motrin),* or if you have a close family history of stomach cancer. (Symptoms of ulcers include a dull, gnawing ache below the breast bone that typically eases during meals, worsens one to three hours later, and intensifies during the night.)

Killing *H. pylori* usually requires a combination of antibiotics and an acid reducer such as lansoprazole *(Prevacid)* or omeprazole *(Prilosec).* If those medications fail, a more invasive examination of the stomach and upper intestine may be required to rule out other conditions, followed by a different combination of antibiotics.

## EATING AROUND ULCERS

**Q** *I have a duodenal ulcer. What foods and beverages should I avoid?*

**A** The usual advice is to avoid foods containing substances that are capable of increasing stomach acid, such as caffeine and alcohol, as well as known stomach irritants, such as aspirin and anti-inflammatory drugs. However, it is now known that well over 90 percent of duodenal ulcers are caused by a bacterium called *Helicobacter pylori*. A two-week course of certain antibiotics and an acid reducer can be curative in most instances and can also prevent recurrences, which used to be common.

## FLATULENCE

**Q** *I've recently begun suffering from flatulence. I'm 65 and have no obvious digestive problems. What could be causing this often embarrassing problem?*

**A** It could be the food you eat. Intestinal gas is the price some people pay for good nutrition. Intestinal bacteria can ferment the remnants of certain carbohydrates, thereby producing gas. Likely culprits include bran and whole grains, as well as many fruits and vegetables, such as apples, avocados, beans, broccoli, cabbage, cauliflower, corn, cucumbers, melons, onions, peas, peppers, and radishes. Sometimes milk and other lactose-containing products (ice cream, puddings, custards) are at fault. Try cutting out suspect foods for a while, and see if it helps.

Swallowed air can also produce a small amount of gas. It may help to eat more slowly, chew with your mouth closed, and avoid gulping food. Over-the-counter remedies such as simethicone

*(Gas-X, Mylanta Gas Relief)* and charcoal tablets are not usually very helpful. Flatulence is nothing to worry about unless it's accompanied by a recent change in bowel habits such as constipation or diarrhea. That could indicate an underlying disorder such as an intestinal infection or tumor, irritable bowel syndrome (spastic colon), or poor food absorption.

---

## ✚ *Office* **Visit**

# IRRITABLE BOWEL SYNDROME?

RECENTLY ONE OF MY PATIENTS, a middle-aged social worker, called to tell me excitedly that she had heard about a new drug for irritable bowel syndrome (IBS). For the previous few years, that ailment's symptoms of bloating, stomach pain, and alternating bouts of diarrhea and constipation had made her life miserable for weeks on end, at times even confining her to home.

Our social worker is far from unique. IBS is a source of misery to more than 50 million Americans, most of them women; it's second only to the common cold as a cause of lost work days. In no other common disorder is the doctor-patient relationship more important than in this perplexing condition, requiring empathy and restraint with medication use on the part of the physician and trust and forbearance on the part of the patient. Only a few die-hards in the medical profession still insist that IBS is psychosomatic. The cause of the condition remains unknown, but research over the years has identified clear abnormalities in people who have it.

In one study the majority of IBS patients had a lower pain threshold to distention of the rectum with air, compared with normal control subjects. There also appears to be increased blood flow to the brain's pain centers while the rectum is distended. Nevertheless, measurements show that the actual quantity of intestinal gas in IBS patients complaining of bloating and distention is no different from that in control subjects.

## MAKING THE DIAGNOSIS

There are no everyday tests capable of diagnosing IBS, but there are agreed-upon symptoms:

• Abdominal pain or discomfort, either intermittently or continuously, for at least three months.

• Constipation or diarrhea, along with temporary relief of the belly discomfort after a bowel movement. Some patients have alternating bouts of constipation and diarrhea.

• Bloating or a feeling of distention, a sense of urgency or of incomplete bowel emptying, and passage of mucus.

Symptoms that are not part of the usual IBS picture include rectal bleeding, anemia, fever, weight loss, persistent diarrhea, onset after age 50, and a family history of colon cancer.

Several disorders can mimic IBS. They must always be considered because they require specific treatment for control or cure. These include:

• Lactose intolerance, or inability to convert milk sugar to more digestible sugars.

• Adult celiac disease, an inherited intestinal allergy to gluten, found in wheat, rye, and barley.

• Bacterial bowel infections. These can occur in a chronic form that mimics IBS.

• Early stages of ulcerative colitis, colon cancer, and Crohn's disease (inflammatory bowel disease).

## TREATING IBS SYMPTOMS

Since the root cause of IBS is unknown, all treatments, including drugs, aim at symptom relief.

For constipation, extra fiber can be helpful, either from diet or supplements. Products containing psyllium *(Metamucil)*, poly-carbophyl *(Mitrolan)*, or methylcellulose *(Citrucel)* can increase intestinal motion. So can tegaserod *(Zelnorm)*, which was recently approved by the Food and Drug Administration (FDA) for use in constipation-predominant IBS. Occasional use of over-the-counter laxatives is permissible, but constant use should be avoided, because the more you use, the more you need to use.

For diarrhea-predominant IBS, over-the-counter loperamide *(Imodium A-D)* helps some people. Others respond better to prescription drugs such as diphenoxylate *(Lomotil)* or cholestyramine *(Questran)*, the latter also used to treat high cholesterol. Antispasmodics such as hyoscyamine *(Levsin)* and dicyclomine *(Bentyl)*, or combination products such as atropine, hyoscyamine, phenobarbital, and scopolamine *(Donnatal)* help to relieve spasms. Among the more effective drugs for those with diarrhea and cramping are low doses of tricyclic antidepressants such as amitriptyline *(Elavil)* and nortriptyline *(Pamelor)*. Alosetron *(Lotronex)*, for treatment of diarrheal IBS, is now back on the market, after having been withdrawn in November 2000. Adverse events included severe constipation, a life-threatening condition called ischemic colitis, and probably a few deaths as well. Be extremely wary about the use of this drug. Its return to the market is unprecedented in the history of the FDA.

The mixed type of IBS is the most difficult to treat. All of the above therapies can be used when necessary for the alternating symptoms of constipation and diarrhea. Avoidance of gas-forming foods, such as beans, broccoli, and onions, helps some individuals. Patients are in the best position to recognize which foods seem to precipitate each phase of the disease.

I asked the social worker to come in for a chat. I had to tell her that tegaserod, the drug she'd asked about, was not indicated for her diarrhea-predominant IBS. For the time being, she would have to get along as best she could on her current treatments.

## The Thyroid

### THYROID-PILL DEPENDENCY?

**Q** *I've taken a small dose of thyroid hormone every day for 40 years. My doctor hadn't diagnosed hypothyroidism; he just recommended the medication for chronic fatigue. Should I stop taking it?*

**A** Probably. However, even though you may not have really needed the drug initially, your thyroid gland has adjusted to the supplement by decreasing its normal production of thyroid hormone. So if you go off the drug now, your thyroid gland could take up to six weeks to recover and you might suffer temporary symptoms of hypothyroidism, such as weight gain and sluggishness. Still, it's better to avoid medication when your body can do the job itself. If you're willing to put up with those symptoms for a few weeks, talk to your physician about discontinuing the pills.

---

### HYPOTHYROIDISM OR LAZINESS?

**Q** *I used to be tired all the time, until doctors diagnosed a thyroid tumor. Before removing it, they started me on thyroid-hormone pills, which I continue to take every day. Almost immediately, my fatigue disappeared and hasn't returned. Is it possible that many people who are considered lazy actually have hypothyroidism?*

**A** Not likely. Thirty or so years ago, thyroid hormone was the fashionable treatment for unexplained lethargy. Many people were unnecessarily "pepped up" with thyroid-hormone pills for years, often without a proper diagnosis of hypothyroidism (underactive thyroid gland). Today we know that hypothyroidism is not a common cause of chronic fatigue alone. There are usually other symptoms of hypothyroidism, including coarse scalp hair, intolerance to cold temperatures, constipation, dry skin, hoarseness, muscle cramps, and weight gain.

## UNDERACTIVE THYROID?

*According to information in a popular medical book, I may have an underactive thyroid gland. My hair, skin, eyes, and mouth are very dry; I have puffiness under my eyes, and I'm very sensitive to cold on my back. But a blood test indicates my thyroid is normal. Are there other ways I should be tested for an underactive thyroid?*

Not if you've had the two appropriate blood tests. One measures thyroid hormone itself, and one measures thyroid-stimulating hormone, or TSH. Your symptoms could be caused by many other problems, including dry environment, medical conditions that dry out the eyes, and certain skin diseases.

## GOITERS AND DIET

*I've read that soybeans contain substances that can interfere with thyroid hormones, possibly causing goiters. I like soy milk and tofu, but I'm concerned because I take the thyroid hormone levothyroxine (Synthroid) to treat an underactive thyroid gland. Should I stop eating soy foods?*

No—but you should be careful about when you eat it. Soybeans and certain vegetables such as cabbage, cassava, rutabagas, and turnips contain substances called goitrogens, which tend to inhibit production of thyroid hormones. But the amount of goitrogens in those foods is so small that even with an underactive thyroid, you'd have to eat shovelsful before they caused even a mild problem, let alone goiters, or visibly enlarged thyroid glands. However, soy may interfere with thyroid hormones in a different way: It appears to inhibit the body's absorption of the hormone pills. So you should probably consume soy at least eight hours before or after you take the levothyroxine.

## Vitamins and supplements

### MAD-COW SUPPLEMENTS?

*Q A recent issue mentioned that some dietary supplements contain the animal parts most likely to harbor the mutant protein that causes mad-cow disease. How can I spot those supplements?*

A Check the ingredients label. Any animal tissue in a supplement should be clearly listed there. The most infectious tissues come from the central-nervous and lymphatic systems—including the brain, heart, liver, lungs, spleen, and thymus—as well as from the intestines. They're usually found in glandular supplements, which contain organ extracts from animals that purportedly boost the function of the corresponding human organs. While the risk of contracting mad-cow disease from such supplements is currently very small, you might still want to avoid them, particularly since the evidence of any benefit is tenuous at best.

## SILVER SUPPLEMENTS

*Q Are there any benefits to taking colloidal silver supplements?*

**A** Almost surely none—and silver can be hazardous. The supplements, which contain tiny silver particles suspended in liquid, have been touted as a nutritional supplement for pregnant women and a treatment for allergies, arthritis, cancer, diabetes, and infection. But silver provides no known nutritional benefits. While it does have mild germ-killing powers, it's too weak and too toxic to be used as an antibiotic. And there's no other plausible explanation for how it might fight disease or protect either the fetus or the mother; in fact, increased blood levels of silver during pregnancy have been linked to birth defects. While decades of consuming trace amounts of the mineral found in some foods and drinking water contribute to such elevated levels, supplements are a more likely cause. Possible toxic effects, in addition to birth defects, include a permanent bluish discoloration of the fingernails, gums, skin, and whites of the eyes and, in more severe cases, organ damage and neurologic disorders. In theory, silver may also interfere with certain antibiotics as well as with drugs for hypertension or thyroid disease.

## A BETTER VITAMIN E?

*Q Is it true that a form of vitamin E called gamma-tocopherol is more beneficial than alpha-tocopherol, the form in most pills?*

**A** It's too soon to say. Recent clinical trials have questioned whether supplements containing alpha-tocopherol provide any protection at all against heart disease. And evidence that it may protect against Alzheimer's disease, Parkinson's disease, and prostate cancer remains controversial. Only a few studies have evaluated gamma-tocopherol's effects in humans, and they measured intake from diet, not supplements. Their preliminary findings suggest that the gamma form from foods may offer better protection against heart disease and prostate cancer than the alpha form. (Dietary sources of gamma-tocopherol include peanuts, pecans, and walnuts as well as oils from corn, soybeans, and sesame seeds.) But that doesn't necessarily mean that a gamma-tocopherol supplement would provide similar protection. So until more is known, it's probably not worth paying the typically higher price for gamma supplements.

## COENZYME Q-10 FOR HEART FAILURE

*Q For many years, my husband and I have taken coenzyme Q-10 because it supposedly helps treat congestive heart failure. But I recently read that it doesn't improve heart function. Does it?*

**A** Apparently not, according to the majority of the research. CoQ10, a naturally occurring body chemical, is an important factor in helping cells turn food into energy. All cells need to generate energy, so in theory supplemental CoQ10 might help congestive heart failure by enabling heart-muscle cells to contract more forcefully. In addition, CoQ10 is an antioxidant, so it theoretically may help prevent further weakening of the heart muscle by preventing chemical damage from oxidation. Some older studies on the effect of CoQ10 supplements in heart-failure patients have shown slight improvement. However, all those studies had significant limitations. In contrast, two recent, better-designed clinical trials found no improvement. On balance, the existing evidence does not support the use of CoQ10 for heart failure.

## VITAMIN D AND WINDOW LIGHT

**Q** *In November, you reported that people generally need some sun exposure to maintain adequate vitamin D levels. But does sunlight passing through windows trigger production of vitamin D?*

**A** No. Glass blocks ultraviolet B (UVB) radiation, the type that stimulates vitamin D synthesis by the skin. To get enough of the vitamin, you probably need to briefly expose some skin to direct sunlight a few days a week during the warmer months—unless you take a multivitamin containing D or consume lots of D-fortified milk plus some fatty fish. (Avoid high fatty-fish intake, which may supply excessive amounts of mercury and other toxins.)

However, you can get sunburned through a window. That's because windows don't block UVA, the other harmful type of radiation from sunlight, unless the glass is specially coated or tinted. Like UVB, UVA can cause sunburn and skin aging as well as an increased risk of skin cancer and possibly cataracts and macular degeneration. So apply sunscreen if you're driving or just sitting in front of a window in bright sunlight for more than about 20 minutes in most parts of North America, and less than that in southern states in the U.S.

---

## VEGGIES IN A PILL?

**Q** *I'm enclosing materials about a product called* Juice Plus, *which claims to supply the highly concentrated nutrition of 11 pounds of fruits and vegetables, with many healthy benefits. If these claims are valid, the product would be great. Could you possibly look into it?*

**A** Juice Plus *is a capsule made of powdered freeze-dried fruit and vegetable juices, which the manufacturer's promotional* literature describes as "whole food–based nutrition." Ronald Watson, a nutritional immunology researcher at the University of Arizona College of Medicine and College of Public Health, used a grant from the manufacturer to put 53 volunteers age 60 and over on *Juice Plus* capsules for 80 days and found that their immune function improved slightly. But the grant didn't pay for recruiting a control group; that makes the results less certain. Nor did the study investigate whether slightly enhanced immune function or eating freeze-dried juices would result in better long-term health. Fresh produce, which contains fiber as well as nutrients, has been strongly linked with a reduced risk of heart disease and certain cancers. Watson, along with other experts we've consulted about similar "veggies in a pill" products, says that the best way to get these established health benefits is to eat the real thing.

## ✚ *Office* **Visit**

# IRON OVERLOAD: A COMMON, UNDERDIAGNOSED DISEASE

WHAT DO THESE THREE PATIENTS HAVE IN COMMON?

• A 55-year-old man—not a problem drinker—awaiting a liver transplant because of end-stage cirrhosis of the liver.

• A 42-year-old woman with a year-round tan, worsening diabetes, and premature menopause.

• A 45-year-old man whose heart failure is causing swollen ankles and severe shortness of breath—but whose coronary arteries and heart valves are normal.

They all have serious, and probably preventable, symptoms

stemming from a common, inherited disorder called hemochromatosis, which permits the slow buildup of damaging amounts of iron in the body. Most victims don't have any idea they have the disease until symptoms start occurring in middle age or later. Even then, diagnosis can be delayed because many doctors just don't think of it.

Thanks to years of supplement ads warning of the dire consequences of "iron-poor" blood (anemia), people tend to think of iron as a mineral that you can't have too much of. In truth, a normal diet supplies ample amounts of iron to meet the needs of most healthy people. The only people who might need supplemental iron are women with excessively heavy menstrual bleeding, and people who bleed from their gastrointestinal tract because of disease or drug side effects.

## THE GENETIC CAUSE

The genetic defect involved in hemochromatosis causes people to absorb more iron than normal from their everyday diet. Over many years, that small daily excess builds up in various body organs.

As little as 15 years ago, hemochromatosis was considered an uncommon medical condition. But through advances in genetics we now know that it is common, occurring in about 1 of every 250 people. Population studies have shown that only a small percentage of people with hemochromatosis currently have symptoms. But, since the consequences of untreated hemochromatosis are so severe, anyone with the disorder should receive treatment whether or not symptoms have developed.

## DIAGNOSIS AND TREATMENT

One reason hemochromatosis is so hard to diagnose is that the organs in which iron builds up can vary from patient to patient. The most common trouble spot is the liver, where the gradual accumulation of iron causes scarring (cirrhosis) and, eventually, progressive liver failure.

Iron accumulating in the skin can impart a golden tone that's difficult to distinguish from a suntan. Iron buildup in the heart muscle can weaken contractions and lead eventually to heart failure. Excess iron in the pancreas destroys insulin-producing cells, resulting in diabetes. Iron that accumulates in the pituitary gland can cause premature menopause in women and impotence in men.

Once hemochromatosis is suspected, the first diagnostic clue is a transferrin saturation blood test to measure the concentration of iron in the blood and the level of transferrin, a protein that transports iron. Elevated blood levels of serum ferritin (the protein responsible for iron storage) add further support.

But not everyone with abnormal test results has hemochromatosis. Liver biopsy, once the definitive test, has been replaced by a $250 blood test that directly detects the errant gene responsible for the disease.

Treatment is simple. Newly diagnosed patients have a pint or two of blood withdrawn each week for one to two years, until transferrin saturation levels drop back to normal. After that, blood is withdrawn as needed to maintain normal levels. After treatment begins, organ damage usually stops progressing.

## SHOULD YOU BE SCREENED?

Blood tests for hemochromatosis are not part of the routine blood work included in periodic checkups. Arguments have raged for years over whether they should be, since many people with the condition may never get ill from it.

I believe that one-time screening for hemochromatosis is worthwhile for all adults, because the disease's consequences are serious and irreversible. Ask your physician for a transferrin saturation screening test at your next checkup.

## Water: Diet and safety

### TONIC-WATER TEMPERANCE?

*Q My doctor told me to drink tonic water with quinine to help soothe leg cramps. But an issue of CRH from several years back said the drug quinine is no longer FDA-approved for anything except malaria because of safety concerns. Should I be worried about drinking tonic water?*

A Probably not. The worrisome adverse effects—notably fever, nausea, vomiting, diarrhea, auditory and visual hallucinations, and, rarely, potentially fatal allergic reactions—are uncommon and occur only when people consume the equivalent of the typical drug dosage of quinine. Even if you chose one of the tonic-water brands highest in quinine, you'd have to consistently drink almost two liters a day to reach that dosage. And even then, the risk is small. Note that a few people are sensitive to quinine and shouldn't drink tonic water at all; fortunately, since there's no way to tell beforehand, such sensitivity is rare.

---

### WATER AND DIETING

*Q Some diet programs have you drink 10 glasses of water a day. What's the point?*

A The main reason is to prevent kidney stones. Very-low-calorie diet programs can break down the body's protein stores, resulting in excess uric acid in the blood. When excreted in the urine, the excess acid can lead to kidney stones. Drinking large quantities of fluids dilutes the urine and lessens the likelihood of stones. In addition, drinking water frequently can stop hunger contractions of the stomach and create a temporary sensation of fullness.

## WELL-WATER SAFETY

**Q** *We recently moved to the country. Is well water automatically better for my family than city water, or can it be just as dangerous? Also, now that we're not drinking fluoridated water, what should I do to keep my family's teeth healthy?*

**A** Well water is by no means automatically safer than city water. In fact, for well-run city systems supplied by protected reservoirs, the reverse may be true.

The quality of well water depends on what's in the underground aquifer from which it's drawn. Among potential aquifer pollutants are septic-tank seepage, gasoline from leaking underground tanks, agricultural fertilizers and pesticides, road salt, and industrial wastes. To make certain your well is safe, have the water tested by a reputable laboratory. Your state health department might test your water for you or suggest a lab to do so. Also check with your local water authority to determine whether periodic testing is advisable.

Make sure the initial test covers fluoride, which occurs naturally in some well water. Children under 14 need fluoride to strengthen their developing teeth. If your water doesn't have the optimal amount, your dentist or pediatrician can prescribe drops or chewable tablets. Using fluoridated toothpaste and fluoride rinses is sufficient to protect against tooth decay in most teenagers and adults.

## Weight control

### LATER MEAL, GREATER WEIGHT?

**Q** *I've heard you shouldn't eat a lot before bedtime, because the calories won't be burned off and will turn to fat. Is that true?*

**A** Almost surely not. Only a few small studies have assessed whether the timing of your meals has any effect on your weight—and the results have been inconclusive. For example, the best of those studies found that women who ate most of their day's calories in the evening lost more body fat in the first half of a 12-week exercise program than those who ate most of their calories in the morning. Researchers have no plausible explanation for why that happened. More important, the weight difference disappeared by the second half of the study. However, there is at least one good reason to avoid stuffing yourself shortly before bedtime: It can lead to poorer sleep, since the body is still working hard to digest the food.

### HOW TO STOP LOSING WEIGHT

**Q** *I'm a 62-year-old man who has lost 15 pounds in two months through diet and exercise. I feel great, but when I reach my desired weight, how do I adjust my regimen to avoiding losing more pounds? Should I let my appetite decide when to level off? Or should I increase the calories and fat in my diet?*

**A** First, don't stop exercising: It provides numerous health benefits beyond weight control. As for food, try following your appetite. If you're like most people, your brain will automatically regulate your calorie intake—and thus your weight—by controlling your hunger. However, that self-regulating system doesn't work for everyone, due to differences in metabolism and heredity. If you continue to lose weight, you should see a doctor. If you start gaining weight, you may have to cut back on fat and calories or try to burn more calories by exercising longer or harder.

## MIDDLE-AGE SPREAD

**Q** *What is the best way to control middle-age spread: diet, exercise, or both?*

**A** Both—including exercises to tone muscles and burn fat. People acquire body fat in two distinct patterns. In so-called middle-age spread, fat accumulates in a "spare tire" around the belly, giving you an apple shape. The other distribution is pear-shaped, with fat deposited around the hips rather than the waist. Men are most often "apples"; women, most often "pears."

Exercises that strengthen your stomach muscles, such as sit-ups, can help restrain a bulging belly. But they won't reduce the amount of abdominal fat. The only way to take that fat off and keep it off is to eat fewer calories and do exercises like biking, jogging, swimming, and walking, which burn a lot of calories.

## IS BEING SKINNY RISKY?

**Q** *I don't smoke or have any disease. But my body mass index is in the underweight range. Is that unhealthy?*

**A** Almost surely not. Body mass index (BMI) was devised to measure obesity, and conclusions drawn about thinness have been misleading. The BMI is calculated by multiplying weight in pounds by 705, dividing by height in inches, then dividing by height again. A BMI of 30 and over is considered obese, 25 through 29 overweight, and 20 through 24 ideal. Scores below 20 are considered underweight because studies have linked them to increased risk of premature death. But that's almost certainly because disease, eating disorders, or malnourishment make some people thin, not because thinness make people susceptible to deadly diseases. And while a low BMI may slightly increase your risk of developing osteoporosis, you can counter that by getting enough exercise and calcium. Note that BMI may be misleading in another way: People who have bulky muscles may be classified as overweight even if they have little body fat.

---

## FLABBY ABDOMEN

**Q** *How can a person lose fat from the lower abdomen when the rest of the body is relatively lean?*

**A** There's really no such thing as "spot reduction" exercises that zero in on fat in a specific area. When you work out, you use energy produced by burning fat from all over your body—not just around the muscles doing the most work. So aside from burning a few calories, all that exercises such as sit-ups do is strengthen your abdominal muscles and help hold your gut in.

However, studies do suggest that people losing weight—whether through any sort of exercise, calorie reduction, or both—tend to shed abdominal fat faster than fat from other parts of the body. That's good news, not only for your appearance, but also for your health: Abdominal fat seems to pose a higher risk of coronary heart disease than fat deposited in other areas.

---

## SKINNY PEOPLE, FATTY DIET

**Q** *Since I'm very thin and want to gain weight, I eat plenty of fatty foods. Will my low weight keep my blood-cholesterol levels down despite the high-fat diet?*

**A** No. A high-fat diet can increase blood-cholesterol levels in thin people as well as in heavy people. The body's tendency to convert dietary fat into blood cholesterol is entirely separate from its tendency to deposit that fat on your waist or thighs. To try to gain weight, increase your consumption of a variety of foods, not just fatty ones. But remember that thin people can have just as much trouble gaining weight and keeping it on as most heavy people have losing weight and keeping it off.

## WHY THIN PEOPLE DON'T GAIN

**Q** *Why do some people stay too thin even though they're trying to gain weight?*

**A** Like their heavy counterparts, thin people seem to be programmed to remain close to a certain weight. They might be able to add pounds by cultivating patently unhealthy habits—avoiding exercise and gorging on high-calorie foods. But most thin people who tried to live that dieter's dream would actually find it hard to stay underactive and overindulgent. Eventually, they'd revert to their usual habits and usual weight. Thin people do have another option: muscle-building exercises. But again, the extra weight will be lost if they stop pumping iron.

## CAN DIET SODAS ADD WEIGHT?

**Q** *I know diet sodas have few or no calories. But I seem to gain weight when I drink them. Could that be because they contain more sodium than regular soda and make me retain fluids?*

**A** Diet soda isn't what's making you gain weight. That comes from eating too much or exercising too little. Many diet sodas do have more sodium than regular soda does. A 12-ounce can of *Diet 7-Up*, for example, contains about 70 milligrams of sodium, whereas regular *7-Up* has 32 milligrams. But 70 milligrams isn't a lot. Since American adults consume an average of 3,400 milligrams of sodium a day, you'd have to guzzle lots of diet pop to boost your sodium intake significantly. Even if you did drink so much, the sodium wouldn't make your body retain a noticeable amount of fluid unless you had heart or kidney problems. People on sodium-restricted diets, however, probably shouldn't drink more than one or two cans of soda a day.

---

✚ *Office* **Visit**

---

# UNINTENTIONAL WEIGHT LOSS

LAST YEAR A 28-YEAR-OLD WOMAN was referred to me because of an overactive thyroid gland, or hyperthyroidism. Her symptoms included nervousness, palpitations, tremors—and a weight loss of about 20 pounds over the previous four months. I prescribed a standard medication, but when she came back three weeks later, she had lost still more weight. I increased her dose, but her weight loss continued. Suspicious, I asked her point-blank if she was taking her medicine. She sheepishly confessed that she wasn't. After a lifetime of yo-yo dieting, she explained, her overactive thyroid seemed like a dream come true. Only after my gentle tirade on the possible complications of untreated hyperthyroidism—an irregular heart rhythm capable of causing a stroke, and loss of muscle strength so severe she might end up in a wheelchair—did she finally agree to take the medicine.

While many of us would be just as happy as this patient to magically be able to lose weight while eating whatever we wanted, unintentional weight loss usually heralds an underlying disorder.

Studies show that in about a fourth of people who lose weight without meaning to, no cause is ever found. But regardless of the underlying reason, unintentional weight loss in and of itself has been correlated with increased rates of sickness and death.

## EAT NORMALLY, LOSE WEIGHT

Hyperthyroidism is one of just a handful of disorders that cause people to lose weight even though they're eating as much as they always have, or even more. Diabetes "wastes" calories in the patient's sugar-rich urine. Gastrointestinal problems such as the adult celiac syndrome can cause malabsorption, or excessive excretion of fat (and its associated calories) in the stool. Unintentional weight loss results more commonly from decreased food intake, which in turn stems from other medical or emotional problems.

• **Difficulty eating.** Anything that makes eating unpleasant or painful will result in weight loss. Age often brings a deterioration of smell and taste, two important cues for eating. Gaps in teeth or poorly fitting dentures can impair chewing. Heartburn can result in reduced food intake.

• **Depression.** Depression can reduce appetite all by itself. Some studies show that depression is to blame in as many as one in five cases of unintentional weight loss. Supportive relatives and friends, professional counseling, and community-outreach programs can all help.

- **Cancer.** When patients start losing weight without trying, their first concern is cancer. They're right to worry; unintentional weight loss is frequently the first symptom of cancer, especially cancers of the pancreas, liver, ovary, or kidney, that can reach an advanced stage before causing other symptoms.
- **Infections.** Tuberculosis of unusual sites such as bone marrow or kidney, as well as strep infections of a heart valve, can reach advanced stages without producing any symptoms except marked weight loss. The weight loss that invariably goes along with the end stages of HIV infection is well known.
- **Chronic disease.** Chronic congestive heart failure, in which damaged heart muscle is incapable of pumping sufficient blood to the body, results in a wasting of muscle and fat (often masked by the accumulation of large amounts of water in the body). In people with chronic lung disease, the increased effort of simply breathing burns enough calories to result in weight loss.

## WHY DOES IT HAPPEN?

In many patients with cancer and certain infectious diseases, the amount of weight loss is greater than can be explained by decreased appetite and food intake. In very sick people, basic body chemistry changes significantly. In addition, many abnormal proteins are produced, some of which can increase muscle and fat breakdown, affect immunity, and decrease appetite. In many older people, research suggests, the body's system of regulating food intake changes, causing them to feel full after eating less.

Since many older people, and some younger ones as well, do not realize that they're losing weight, make sure you get your weight recorded at every doctor visit, a simple task that is frequently overlooked. If you find that you've lost more than 5 percent of your weight without trying, it's time for medical investigation to find and treat the reason.

## Women's health

### PAP SMEAR AFTER HYSTERECTOMY

**Q** *My uterus was removed 24 years ago at age 36. All other reproductive organs were left intact. Since that time, I've received conflicting advice about the need to have an annual Pap smear when there's no uterus. Can you clarify?*

**A** If your cervix was left in place when your uterus was removed, you definitely should still have an annual Pap smear to screen for cervical cancer. However, when the cervix is removed along with the uterus, there's no longer any need to have the test. While some doctors perform Pap smears even in those women to screen for vaginal cancer, that form of cancer is extremely rare and doesn't warrant an annual smear.

---

### ANNUAL PAP SMEAR

**Q** *How often should a woman get a Pap smear? And what time of month gives the most accurate results?*

**A** The venerable Pap smear is one of the most important cancer-detection tests. A woman should begin having an annual Pap smear by age 21 (or earlier, if she is sexually active) through age 30. Then either the Pap smear every two to three years after three consecutive normal results, or both the test for Pap smear and the human papillomavirus (HPV, a virus that causes cervical cancer) every three years after one normal result on both tests. Some gynecologists recommend that women at high risk for cervical cancer be tested even more frequently. (Risk factors include multiple sex partners, certain viruses, venereal warts, and smoking.) Pap smears should not be done during the menstrual period. Some recent data suggest that the test is more accurate during the first half of the cycle if you use oral contraceptives. Midcycle is preferred for most other menstruating women. Regardless of the timing, the technician reading the smear must know if you're taking oral contraceptives or estrogen replacement therapy, and the date of your last menstrual period.

## SOY AND BREAST CANCER

**Q** *I have read that the plant estrogens in soybeans may not be safe for postmenopausal women. My oncologist "felt" that consuming soy was "probably" OK. But having had breast cancer, I don't want to follow feelings or "probably."*

**A** There's not enough hard evidence to make a definitive statement about the health effects of soy-based estrogens. Several observational studies have found that women who consumed the most plant-based estrogens have a lower risk of breast cancer than women who consumed the least. But there's also at least a theoretical concern that those compounds may stimulate tumor growth in women who have estrogen-responsive breast cancer, particularly postmenopausal women.

The overall pattern of your diet matters more than any one particular food. It's probably OK for women—including postmenopausal women with breast cancer—to eat soy-based foods in moderate amounts as part of a balanced diet (low in animal fat, high in produce). However, our consultants feel that those women—as well as women at high risk for breast cancer—should talk with their doctors before consuming large amounts of soy.

## BREAST TENDERNESS

**Q** *For breast tenderness, my gynecologist recommended 1,200 IU of vitamin E a day for life. He also recommended cutting back on caffeine. Are those treatments effective?*

**A** There's no convincing evidence that eliminating caffeine or adding vitamin E helps relieve breast pain, which is usually caused by fluid retained just before menstruation. If your pain does precede menstruation, you might try taking a mild diuretic during the few days before your period. An over-the-counter pain reliever and a supportive bra might also help.

## HOT FLASHES AND DIURETICS

**Q** *I've heard that the water-ridding properties of diuretics such as* Dyazide *[triamterene/hydrochlorothiazide] make it essential to drink plenty of fluids during hot weather to prevent dehydration. Since the hot flashes that accompany menopause can also make you sweat, would that likewise lead to a dehydration risk from diuretics?*

**A** No. Menopausal hot flashes are caused by temporarily dilated blood vessels in the skin. While that may make you sweat, you won't lose a significant amount of water, even if you're taking a diuretic.

## HUNCHED BACK

**Q** *I'm a 63-year-old woman and am starting to develop a hunched back. Is there some exercise to delay that?*

**A** No. Your problem is probably osteoporosis, or bone thinning, which commonly follows menopause. The weakened spinal vertebrae simply fracture and collapse. You should consult your physician about the first-line drug treatment options for osteoporosis, which include alendronate *(Fosamax)*, raloxifene *(Evista)*, risedronate *(Actonel)*, or the nasal spray calcitonin *(Miacalcin)*. Weight-bearing exercises, daily intake of 400 to 800 I.U. vitamin D, and 1,200 milligrams elemental calcium should be basic treatment for osteoporosis.

## OVARIAN CANCER CLUE?

**Q** *I have heard on two television talk shows about a screening test for early diagnosis of ovarian cancer. What is the test and is it effective?*

**A** A blood test called CA-125 is being used to monitor the treatment of women with ovarian cancer and to check for recurrence. The test is very sensitive but not specific: It can detect ovarian cancer, but it also can turn up positive in the presence of other conditions, including pregnancy, endometriosis, uterine fibroids, and pelvic inflammatory disease. For that reason, many physicians do not use CA-125 as a screening test for ovarian cancer unless a woman is at high risk because of family history. Such a woman should have a CA-125 blood test annually and should discuss with her physician the suitability of having an annual transvaginal ultrasound examination of the ovaries. In a few years the results of a major cancer screening trial may very well provide better answers as to just how effective the CA-125 test is at detecting ovarian cancer in all women.

## THE PILL WITHOUT WEIGHT GAIN?

**Q** *I've read that the new birth-control pill* Yasmin, *unlike previous pills, can help control your weight. Is that true?*

**A** It's too soon to tell. Preliminary studies have found that women taking drospirenone plus ethinyl estradiol *(Yasmin)* either lost more weight or gained less than those taking other contraceptive pills. But the average differences were very small, and further studies are needed to confirm the findings. Moreover, drospirenone can cause potassium retention, which may be worrisome in women who have kidney disease or are taking any of these antihypertensive drugs: potassium-sparing diuretics such as spironolactone *(Aldactone)* and triamterene *(Dyazide, Maxzide)*; ACE inhibitors such as lisinopril *(Prinivil, Zestril)*, quinapril *(Accupril)*, and ramipril *(Altace)*; and angiotensin-receptor blockers such as candesartan *(Atacand)*, losartan *(Cozaar)*, and valsartan *(Diovan)*. If you want an oral contraceptive, you should probably stick with an older pill whose safety is better established, such as norgestrel *(Lo/Ovral)* or norgestimate *(Ortho Tri-Cyclen)*, both of which are combined with ethinyl estradiol.

---

## CONTRACEPTION ALERT

**Q** *Is it true that the antibiotic tetracycline* (Achromycin) *can reduce the effectiveness of birth-control pills?*

**A** Yes. So can a long list of other common drugs (and even an herb). Those include the antibiotics amoxicillin *(Amoxil, Polymox, Trimox, Wymox)*, ampicillin *(Principen, Totacillin)*, doxycycline *(Vibramycin)*, penicillin *(Betapen, Ledercillin, V-Cillin)*, and rifampin *(Rifadin, Rimactane)*; the anticonvulsant drugs carbamazepine *(Atretol, Carbatrol, Epitol, Tegretol)*, phenytoin *(Dilantin, Phenytex)* and primidone *(Myidone, Mysoline)*; the antifungal medication griseofulvin *(Fulvicin, Grifulvin, Grisactin)*; and the antidepressant herb St. John's wort. All those agents can boost the production of certain liver enzymes that help the body eliminate estrogens, which are the active ingredients in many birth-control pills. So in theory, they could all reduce protection against pregnancy. In practice, unintentional pregnancies have been reported in women taking certain of those medications together with the pill. To be safe, use an alternative or additional form of birth control if you're taking any of these agents while using an oral contraceptive.

---

## ANTIBIOTICS AND YEAST

**Q** *Every time I take antibiotics, I end up with a yeast infection. How can I prevent this?*

**A** Whether or not yeast infections can be prevented is a matter of controversy. Since you always seem to get an infection when taking antibiotics, you could try using an antifungal vaginal cream at the same time. Those creams include butoconazole *(Femstat 3)*, clotrimazole *(FemCare, Gyne-Lotrimin)*, and miconazole *(Monistat 3)*, all sold over the counter.

---

# Index